FOREWORD

I started out in this business as a fan. I loved comics with a passion, spent far too much time and money on them, wrote for fanzines, went to conventions, made friends with other comic fans and finally ended up writing and drawing my own comics. The transition from fan to professional was a gradual one and there certainly wasn't a day when I woke up feeling like a pro, or for that matter, when I stopped being a fan. I get the feeling that Greg is following a similar path, doing what he loves, telling stories whether he gets paid for it or not, and one day soon he's going to realize that there is no escape - he'll be doing this for the rest of his life.

I've known Greg for ten years now, since I first corresponded with him on the Spawn message boards. Todd McFarlane and Spawn-editor Brian Haberlin had given me my first long-term scripting gig on the monthly Spawn book after I had cut my teeth on a couple of shorter runs on Marvel books. They encouraged me to be active on the Spawn message board. This was the first time I had really had online interaction with comic fans and it was one hell of an experience. Spawn fans were just that – fanatics! Using the name Dan Kane, Greg was one of the most prolific and enthusiastic posters, arguing, critiquing and giving up the love for all things Spawn. The conversations were really good for me. It made the creative process a two-way channel between writer and reader. The feedback was so fast, so well-informed, that it actually did influence the direction of the comic's plot and character development.

We talked for years on the message board without meeting in person. For an old fogey like me the concept of an online friendship was something I resisted. "Online friends aren't real friends!" Except sometimes they are. When we finally did meet up at the New York Comic Con it really did feel like running into an old friend and I found that Greg has been progressing along that same path that I did, developing his skills, making stories, writing comics, acting, directing, modeling... Wait! Acting? Modelling?! Okay, hold up, here's where I have to admit to a degree of envy. I never did much outside of comic books and to see Greg writing theatre, making movies, active as an online journalist...there's an energy and a thirst for creative diversity that is genuinely impressive. That breadth of experience is already showing through in the writing and the way he gets under the skin of the characters.

In Is'nana: The Werespider, Greg is creating a new mythology of horror, rooted in the Vodun religion of West Africa, filtered through the modern American superhero mythology of the Spider-Man and (of course) Spawn, this is a story about the primal human embodied in those legends and how the sophistication and complexity of modern living actually obscures and restrains human nature.

Yes, it's a twisted horror story with some truly memorable and nightmarish images - Is'nana's spider-father sitting on his shoulder like some freakish Jiminy Cricket, Osebo taking possession of his human victim, and the scariest-looking hero since... well no, actually in his Anansi guise, this hero is actually more terrifying than even Spawn ever was. But here's what's important and what makes this a great story...there is warmth and empathy for the characters. Behind the horror, the story is about surviving the worst that life can throw at you, while keeping your humanity. It's about the hunger for intimacy and the search for love. And above all it's about the knowledge that we are all part of one vast inter-linked narrative. To quote Greg's own words: "Stories. That is all that is. Stories. It is what we are and will become..."

This story is just beginning...

David Hine

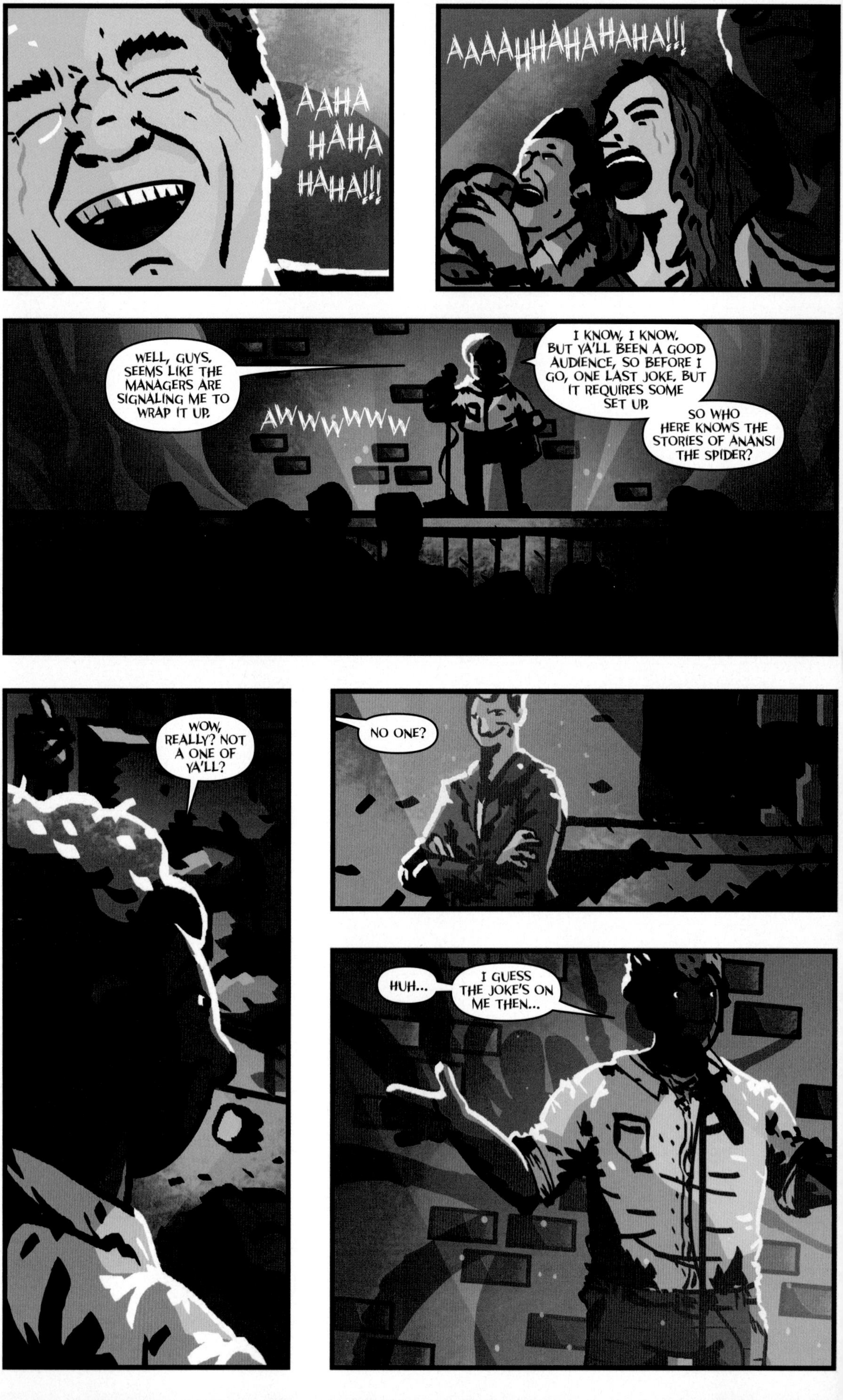
AAHA HAHA HAHA!!!
AAAAHHAHAHAHA!!!
WELL, GUYS, SEEMS LIKE THE MANAGERS ARE SIGNALING ME TO WRAP IT UP.
AWWWWWWW
I KNOW, I KNOW. BUT YA'LL BEEN A GOOD AUDIENCE, SO BEFORE I GO, ONE LAST JOKE. BUT IT REQUIRES SOME SET UP.
SO WHO HERE KNOWS THE STORIES OF ANANSI THE SPIDER?
WOW, REALLY? NOT A ONE OF YA'LL?
NO ONE?
HUH...
I GUESS THE JOKE'S ON ME THEN...

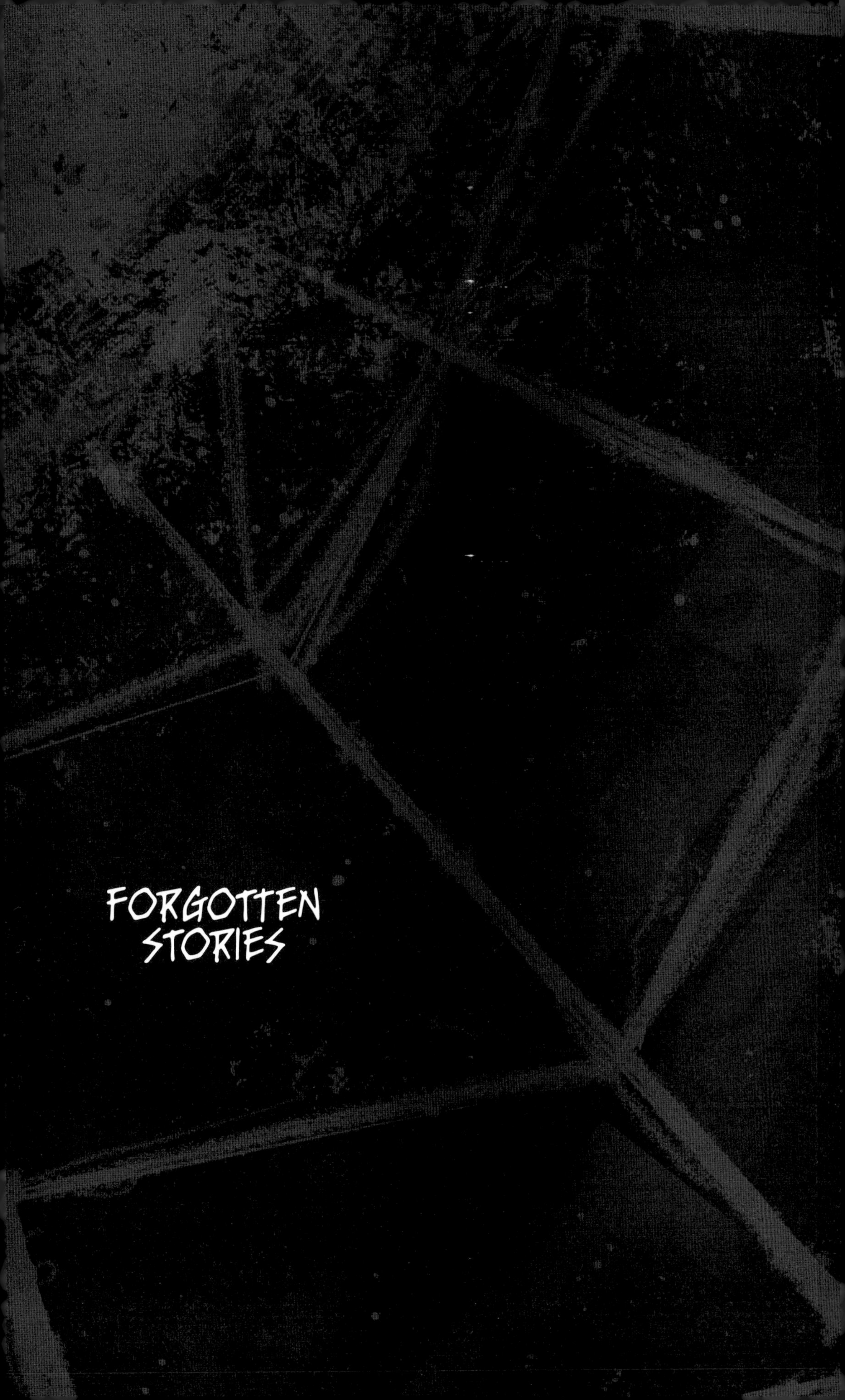

FORGOTTEN
STORIES

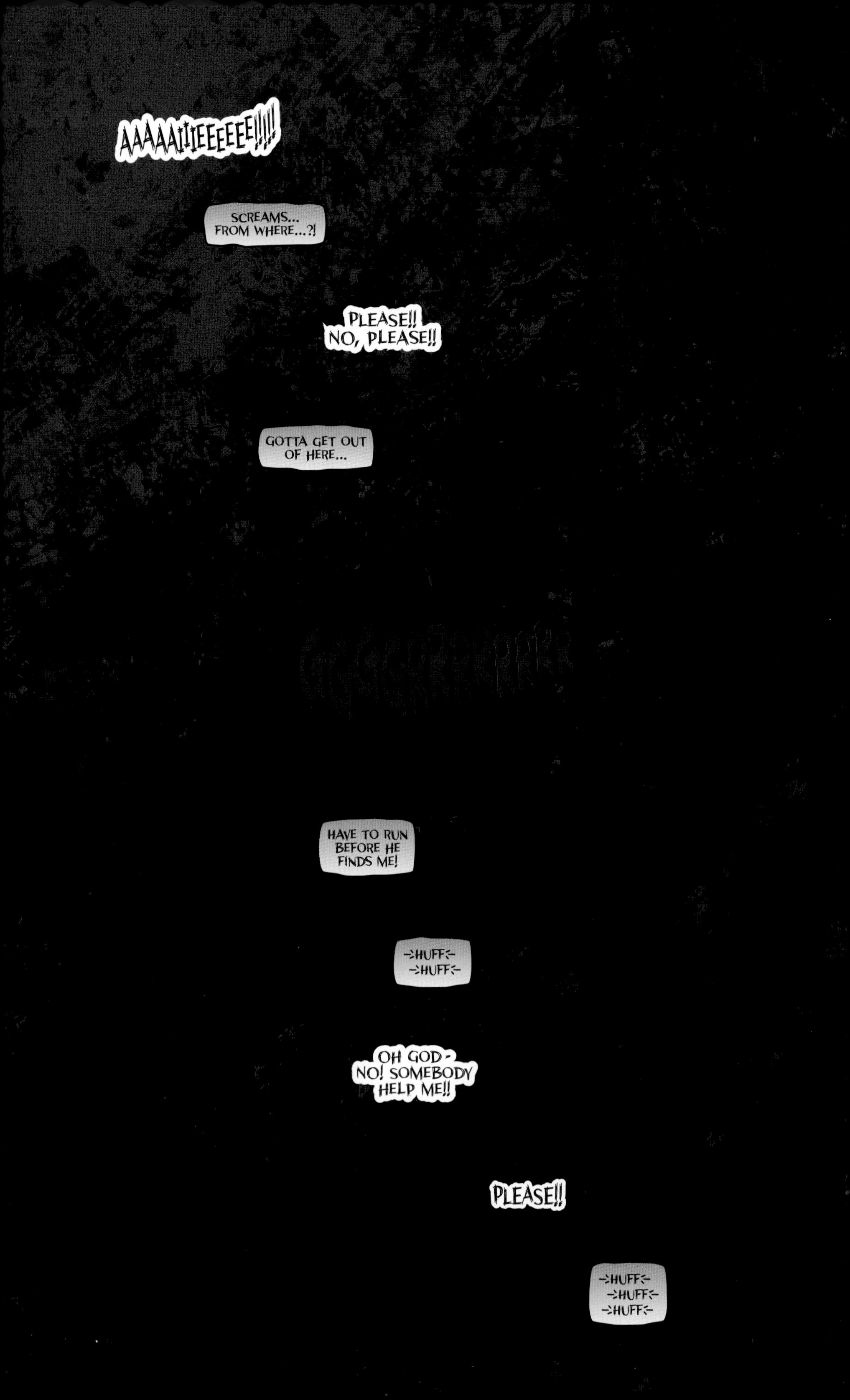
AAAAAIIIIEEEEEE!!!!!
SCREAMS... FROM WHERE...?!
PLEASE!! NO, PLEASE!!
GOTTA GET OUT OF HERE...
HAVE TO RUN BEFORE HE FINDS ME!
-HUFF- -HUFF-
OH GOD - NO! SOMEBODY HELP ME!!
PLEASE!!
-HUFF- -HUFF- -HUFF-

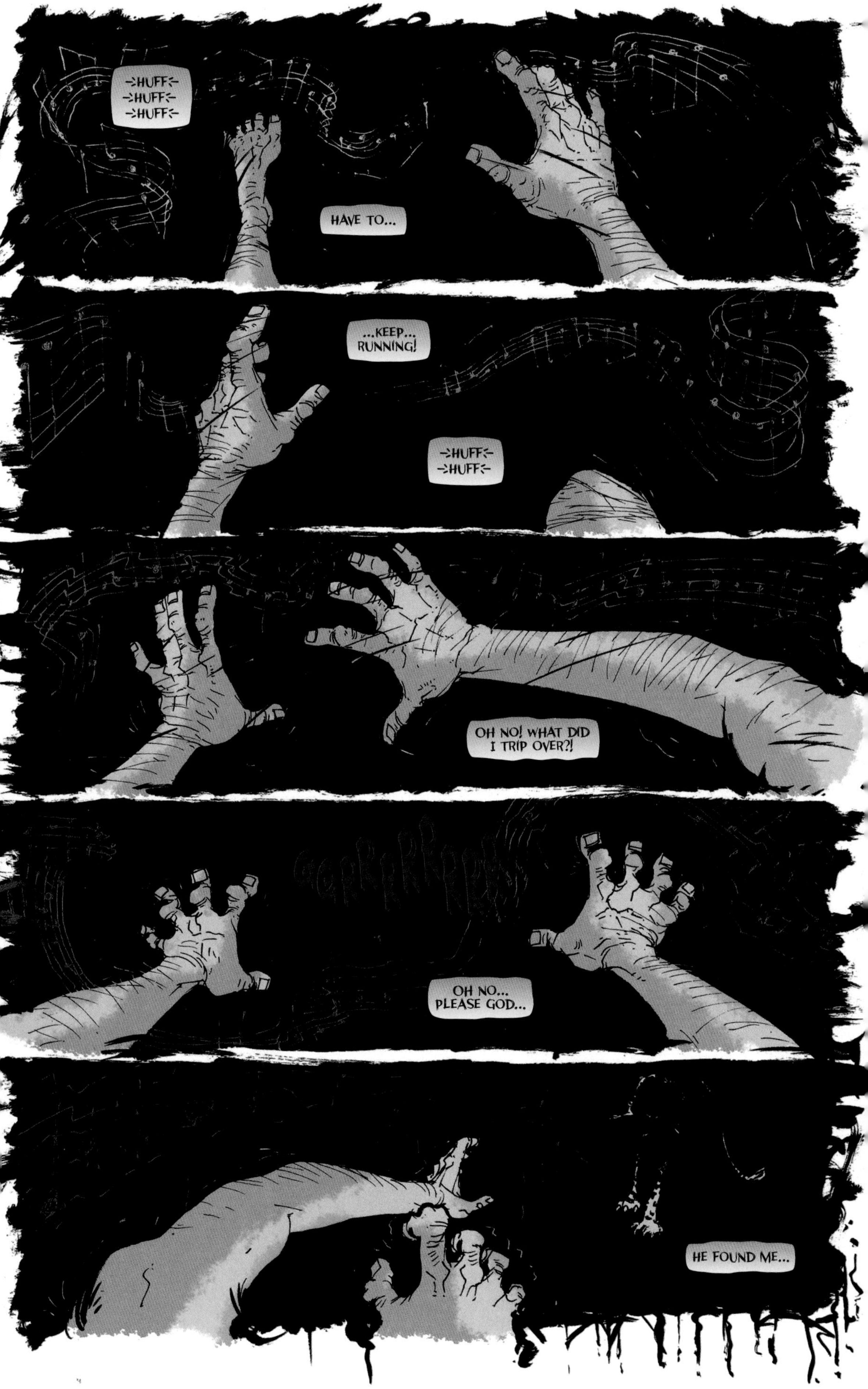

HUFF HUFF HUFF
HAVE TO...
...KEEP... RUNNING!
HUFF HUFF
OH NO! WHAT DID I TRIP OVER?!
OH NO... PLEASE GOD...
HE FOUND ME...

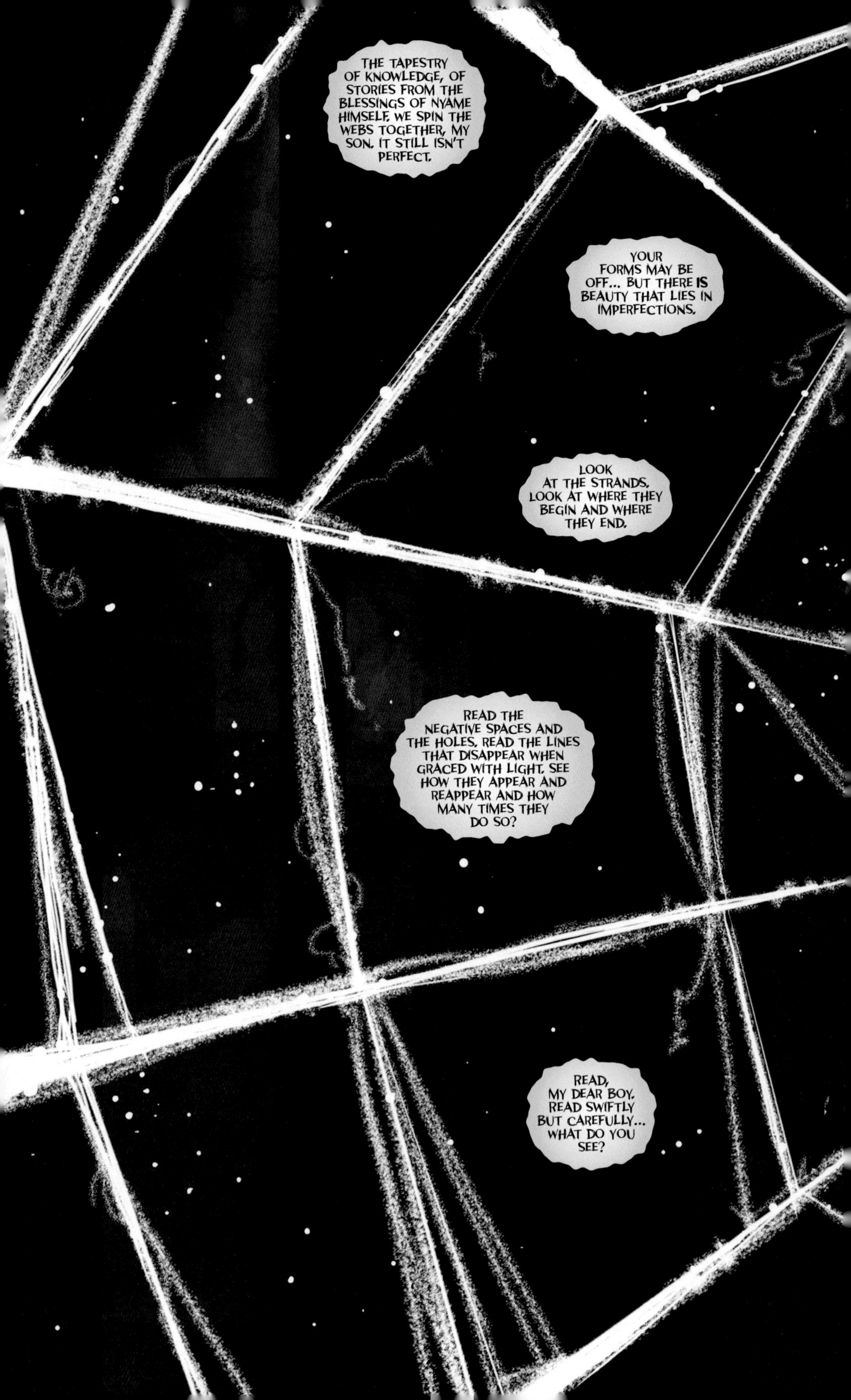
THE TAPESTRY OF KNOWLEDGE, OF STORIES FROM THE BLESSINGS OF NYAME HIMSELF. WE SPIN THE WEBS TOGETHER, MY SON. IT STILL ISN'T PERFECT.
YOUR FORMS MAY BE OFF... BUT THERE IS BEAUTY THAT LIES IN IMPERFECTIONS.
LOOK AT THE STRANDS. LOOK AT WHERE THEY BEGIN AND WHERE THEY END.
READ THE NEGATIVE SPACES AND THE HOLES. READ THE LINES THAT DISAPPEAR WHEN GRACED WITH LIGHT. SEE HOW THEY APPEAR AND REAPPEAR AND HOW MANY TIMES THEY DO SO?
READ, MY DEAR BOY. READ SWIFTLY BUT CAREFULLY... WHAT DO YOU SEE?

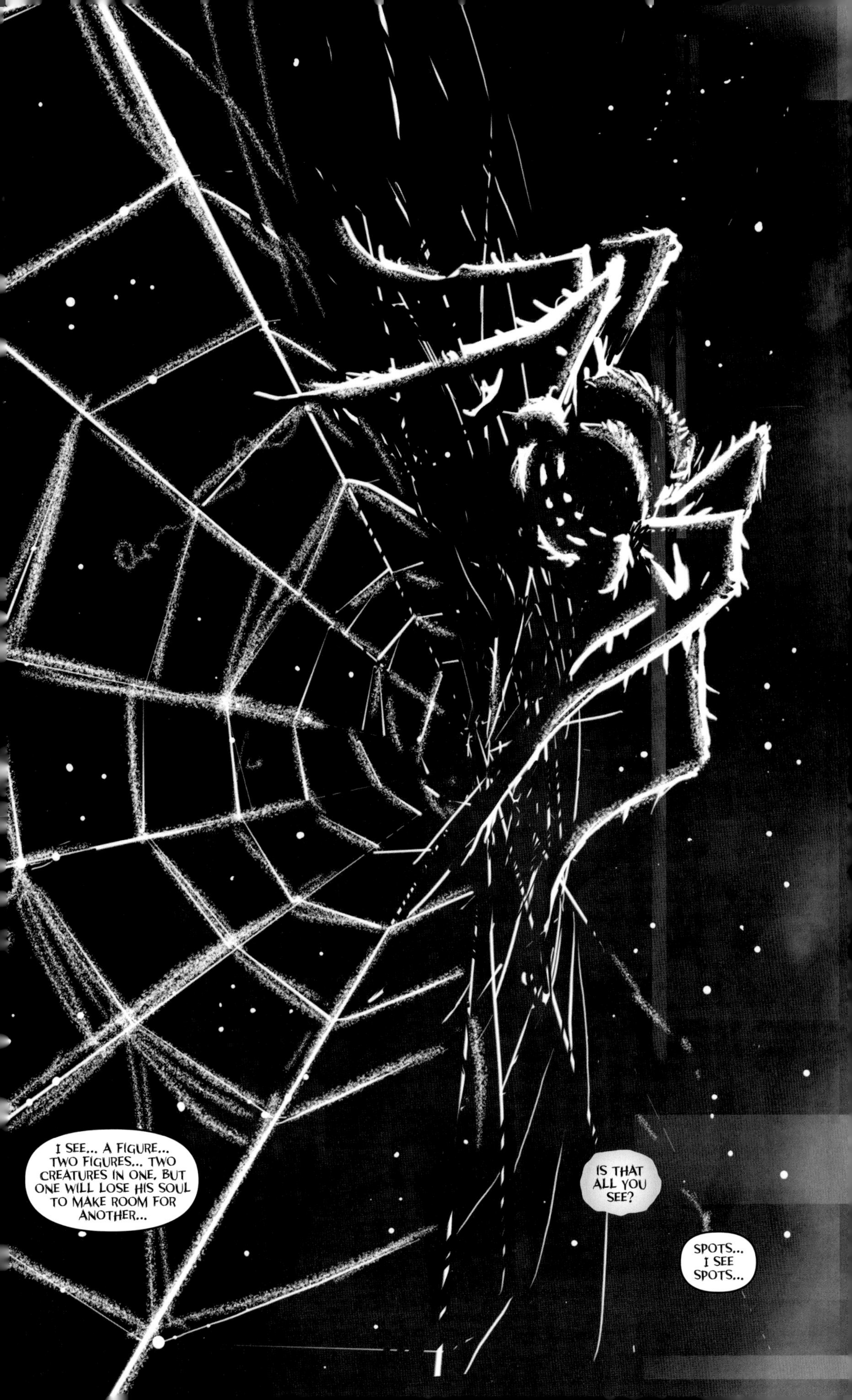
I SEE... A FIGURE... TWO FIGURES... TWO CREATURES IN ONE, BUT ONE WILL LOSE HIS SOUL TO MAKE ROOM FOR ANOTHER...
IS THAT ALL YOU SEE?
SPOTS... I SEE SPOTS...

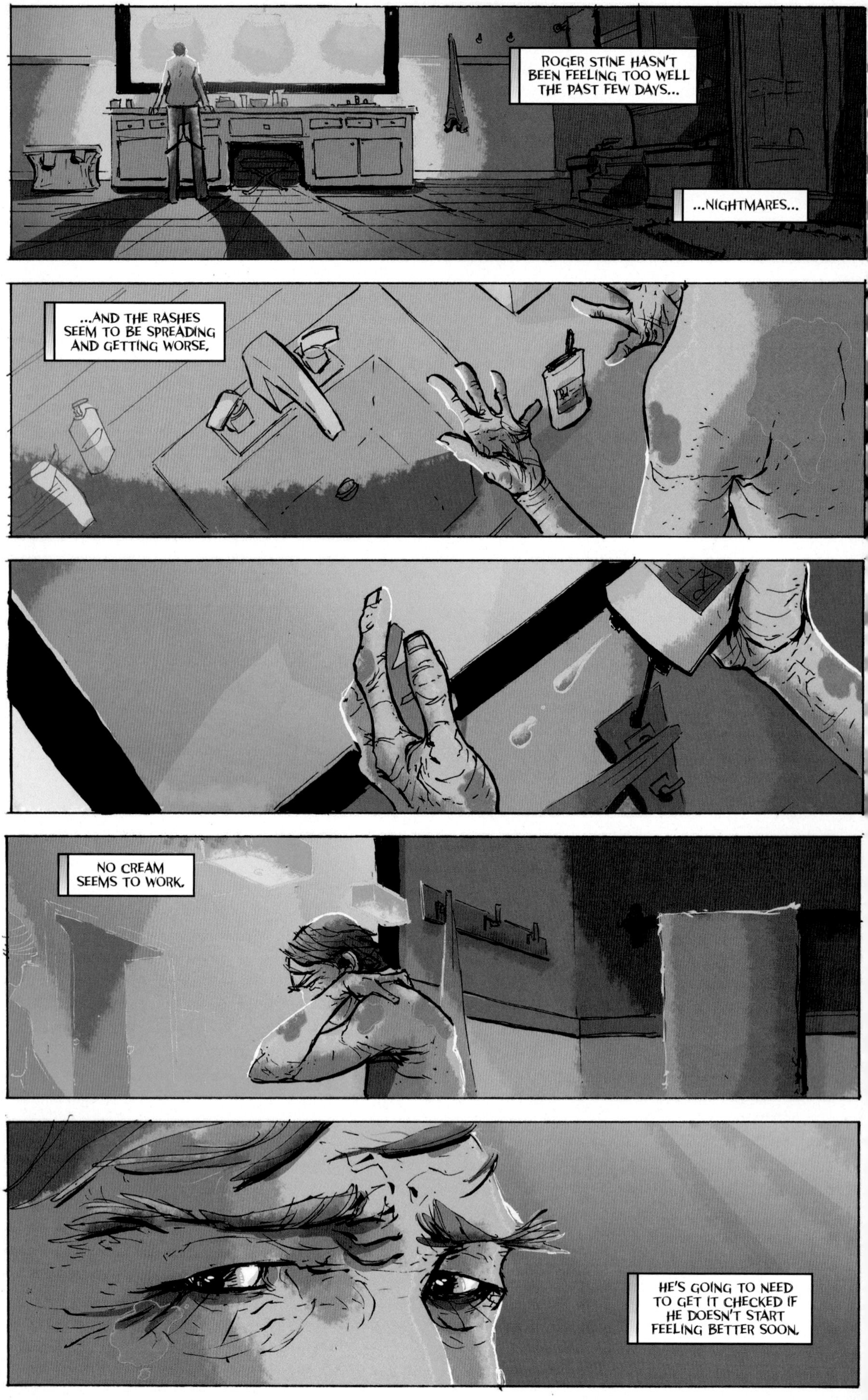
ROGER STINE HASN'T BEEN FEELING TOO WELL THE PAST FEW DAYS...
...NIGHTMARES...
...AND THE RASHES SEEM TO BE SPREADING AND GETTING WORSE.
NO CREAM SEEMS TO WORK.
HE'S GOING TO NEED TO GET IT CHECKED IF HE DOESN'T START FEELING BETTER SOON.

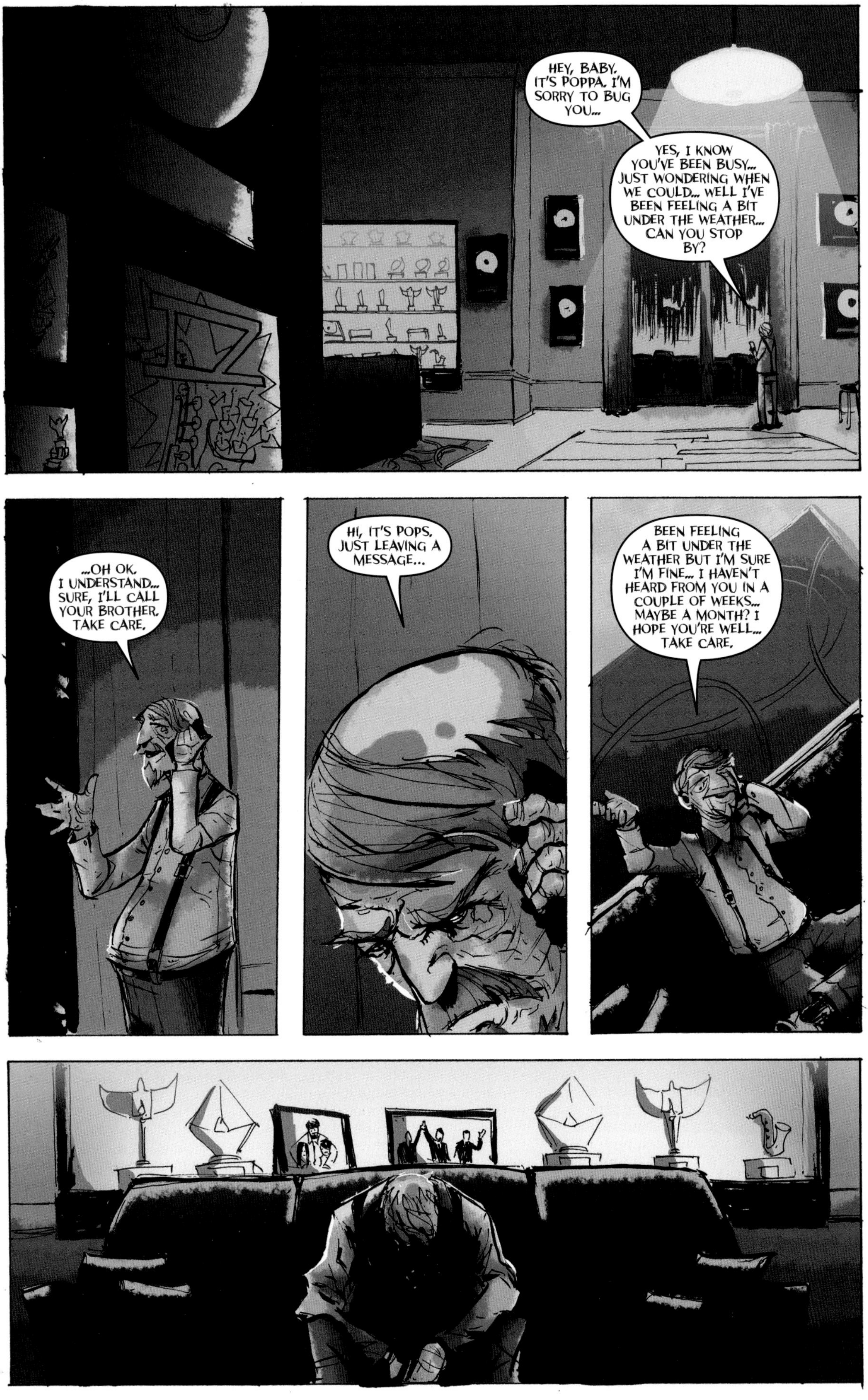
HEY, BABY. IT'S POPPA. I'M SORRY TO BUG YOU...
YES, I KNOW YOU'VE BEEN BUSY... JUST WONDERING WHEN WE COULD... WELL I'VE BEEN FEELING A BIT UNDER THE WEATHER... CAN YOU STOP BY?
...OH OK. I UNDERSTAND... SURE, I'LL CALL YOUR BROTHER. TAKE CARE.
HI, IT'S POPS. JUST LEAVING A MESSAGE...
BEEN FEELING A BIT UNDER THE WEATHER BUT I'M SURE I'M FINE... I HAVEN'T HEARD FROM YOU IN A COUPLE OF WEEKS... MAYBE A MONTH? I HOPE YOU'RE WELL... TAKE CARE.

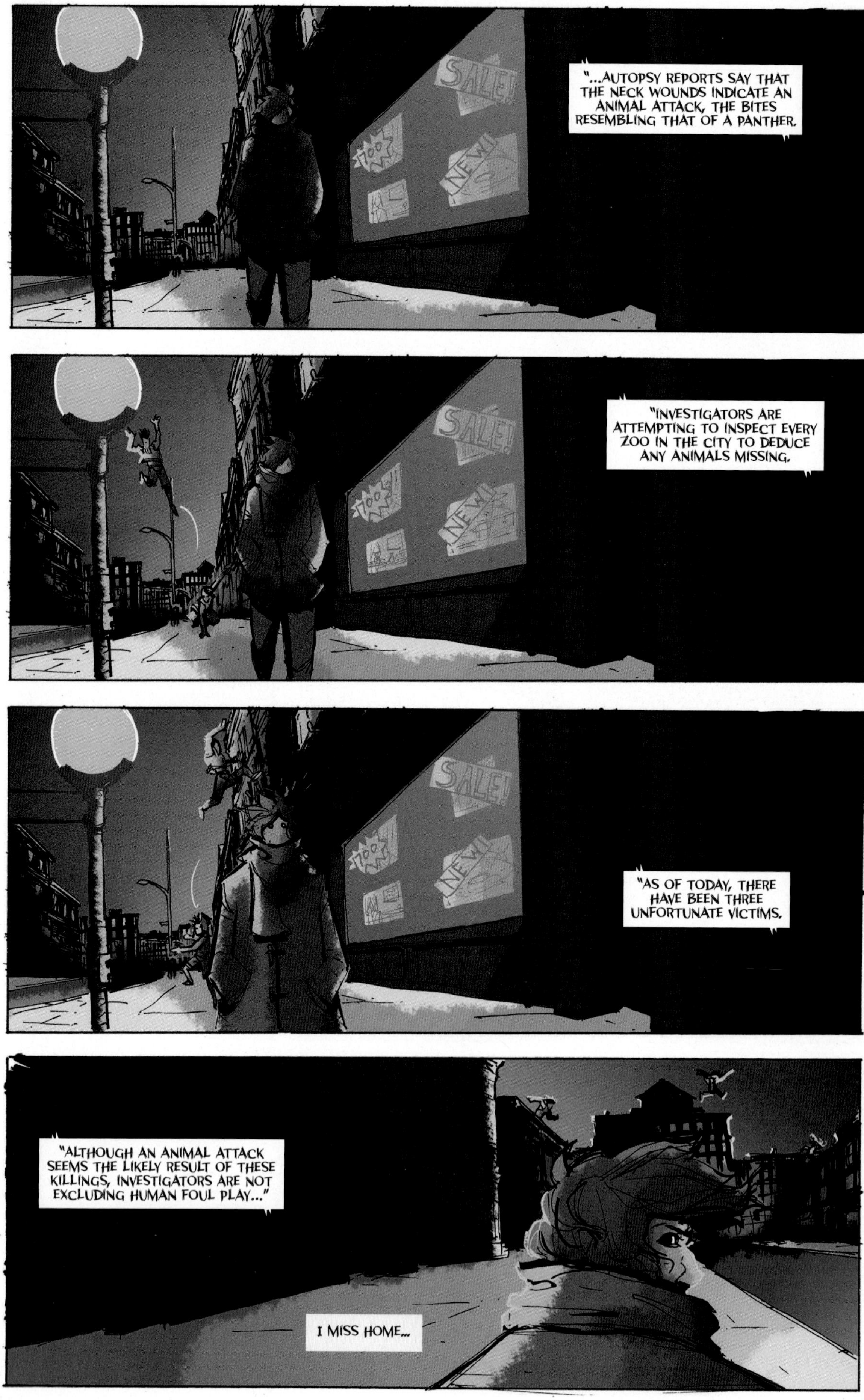
SALE!
NEW!
"...AUTOPSY REPORTS SAY THAT THE NECK WOUNDS INDICATE AN ANIMAL ATTACK, THE BITES RESEMBLING THAT OF A PANTHER.
"INVESTIGATORS ARE ATTEMPTING TO INSPECT EVERY ZOO IN THE CITY TO DEDUCE ANY ANIMALS MISSING.
"AS OF TODAY, THERE HAVE BEEN THREE UNFORTUNATE VICTIMS.
"ALTHOUGH AN ANIMAL ATTACK SEEMS THE LIKELY RESULT OF THESE KILLINGS, INVESTIGATORS ARE NOT EXCLUDING HUMAN FOUL PLAY..."
I MISS HOME...

...I MISS THE TALL TREES AND THE COLORS ILLUMINATED BY THE HOT SUN.

I MISS MY FRIENDS AND I MISS MAMA AND HER COOKING. I MISS GRANDFATHER NYAME AND HIS THUNDERING LAUGHS.

I MISS RUNNING THROUGH THE DIRT AND FEELING IT BETWEEN MY TOES,

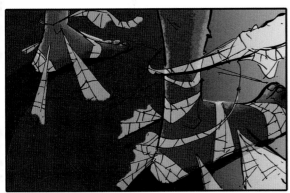

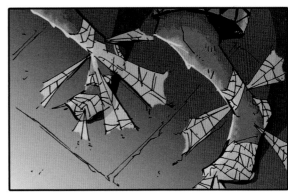

AND SPINNING WEBS WITH MY FRIENDS AND WRESTLING WITH BR'ER LIL RABBIT.

IN THIS PLACE I SEE HUMANS WALKING AND SPENDING THEIR DAYS BEING CHIPPED FURTHER AWAY FROM THEIR ESSENCE...

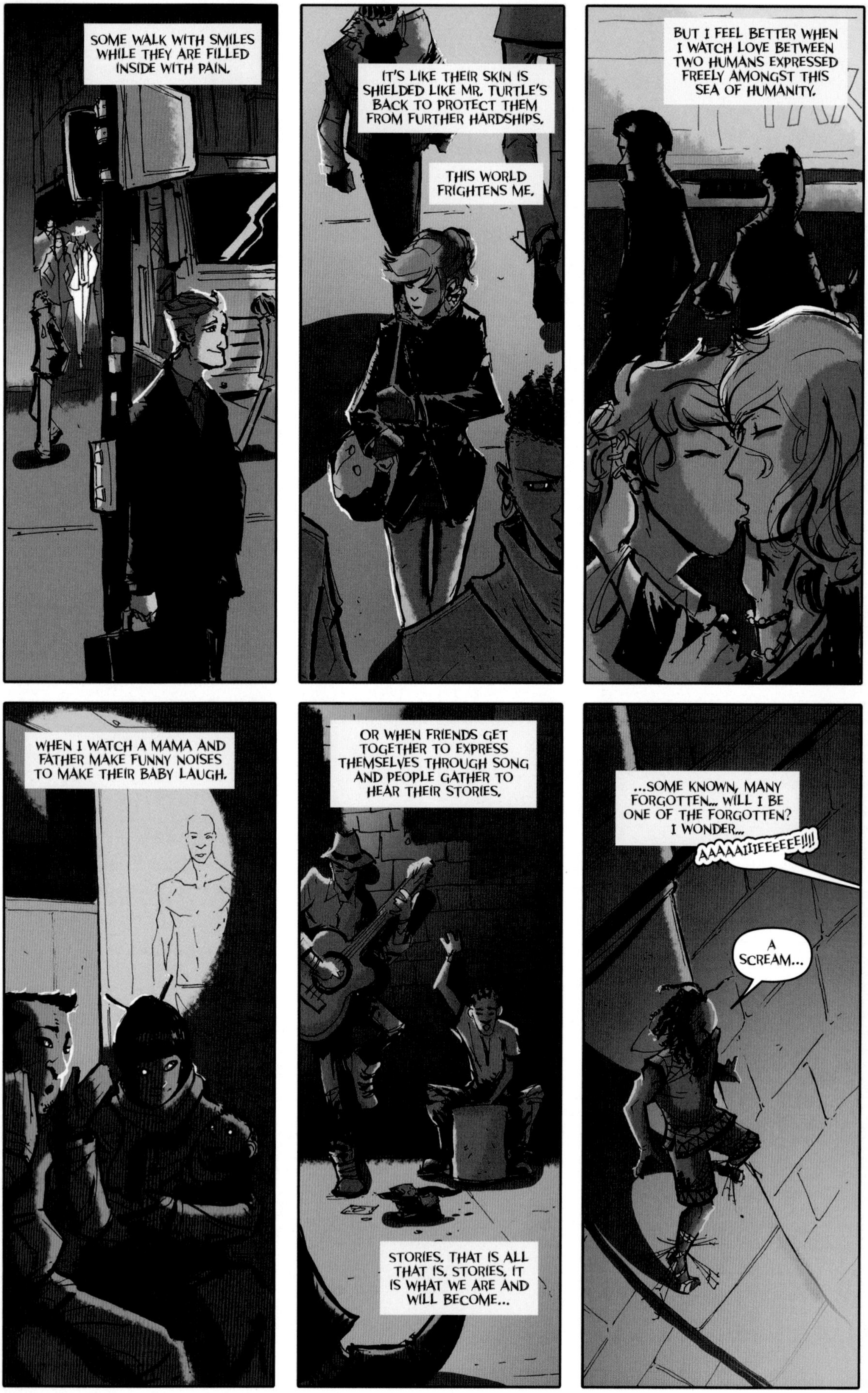
SOME WALK WITH SMILES WHILE THEY ARE FILLED INSIDE WITH PAIN.
IT'S LIKE THEIR SKIN IS SHIELDED LIKE MR. TURTLE'S BACK TO PROTECT THEM FROM FURTHER HARDSHIPS.
THIS WORLD FRIGHTENS ME.
BUT I FEEL BETTER WHEN I WATCH LOVE BETWEEN TWO HUMANS EXPRESSED FREELY AMONGST THIS SEA OF HUMANITY.
WHEN I WATCH A MAMA AND FATHER MAKE FUNNY NOISES TO MAKE THEIR BABY LAUGH.
OR WHEN FRIENDS GET TOGETHER TO EXPRESS THEMSELVES THROUGH SONG AND PEOPLE GATHER TO HEAR THEIR STORIES.
STORIES. THAT IS ALL THAT IS. STORIES. IT IS WHAT WE ARE AND WILL BECOME...
...SOME KNOWN, MANY FORGOTTEN... WILL I BE ONE OF THE FORGOTTEN? I WONDER...
AAAAAIIIEEEEEE!!!!
A SCREAM...

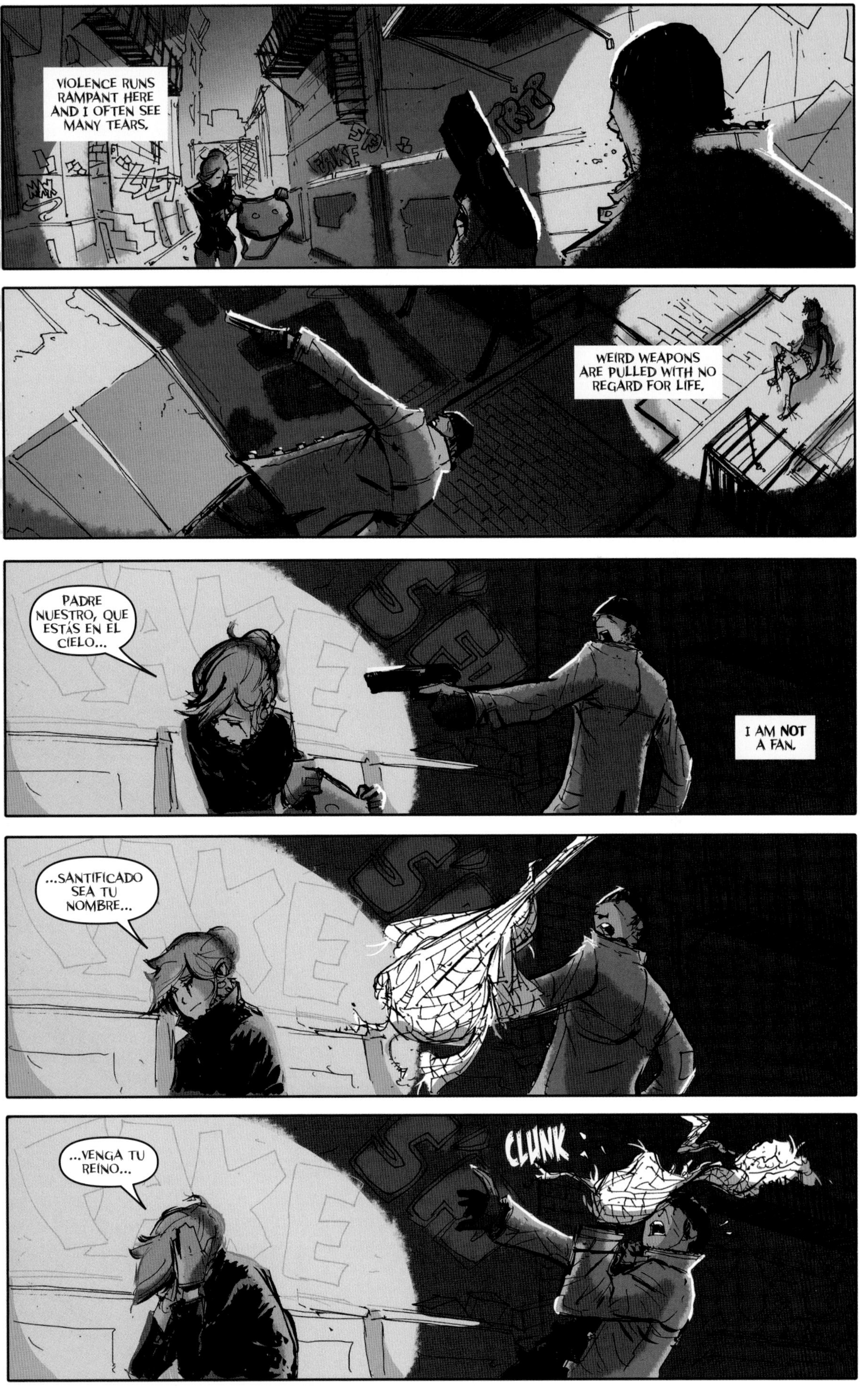
VIOLENCE RUNS RAMPANT HERE AND I OFTEN SEE MANY TEARS.
FAKE
WEIRD WEAPONS ARE PULLED WITH NO REGARD FOR LIFE.
PADRE NUESTRO, QUE ESTÁS EN EL CIELO...
I AM NOT A FAN.
...SANTIFICADO SEA TU NOMBRE...
...VENGA TU REINO...
CLUNK

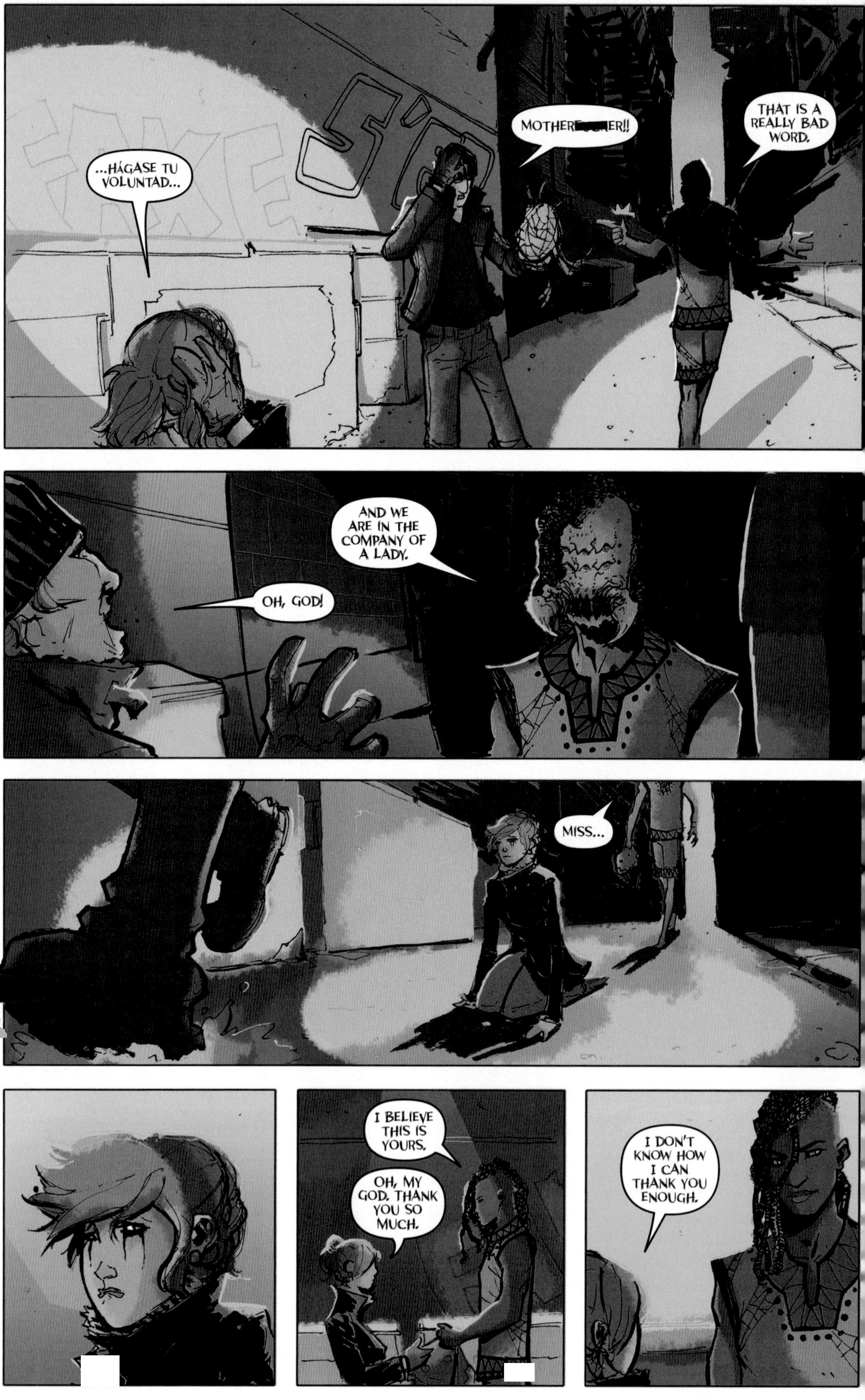

...HÁGASE TU VOLUNTAD...
MOTHER[redacted]ER!!
THAT IS A REALLY BAD WORD.
AND WE ARE IN THE COMPANY OF A LADY.
OH, GOD!
MISS...
I BELIEVE THIS IS YOURS.
OH, MY GOD. THANK YOU SO MUCH.
I DON'T KNOW HOW I CAN THANK YOU ENOUGH.

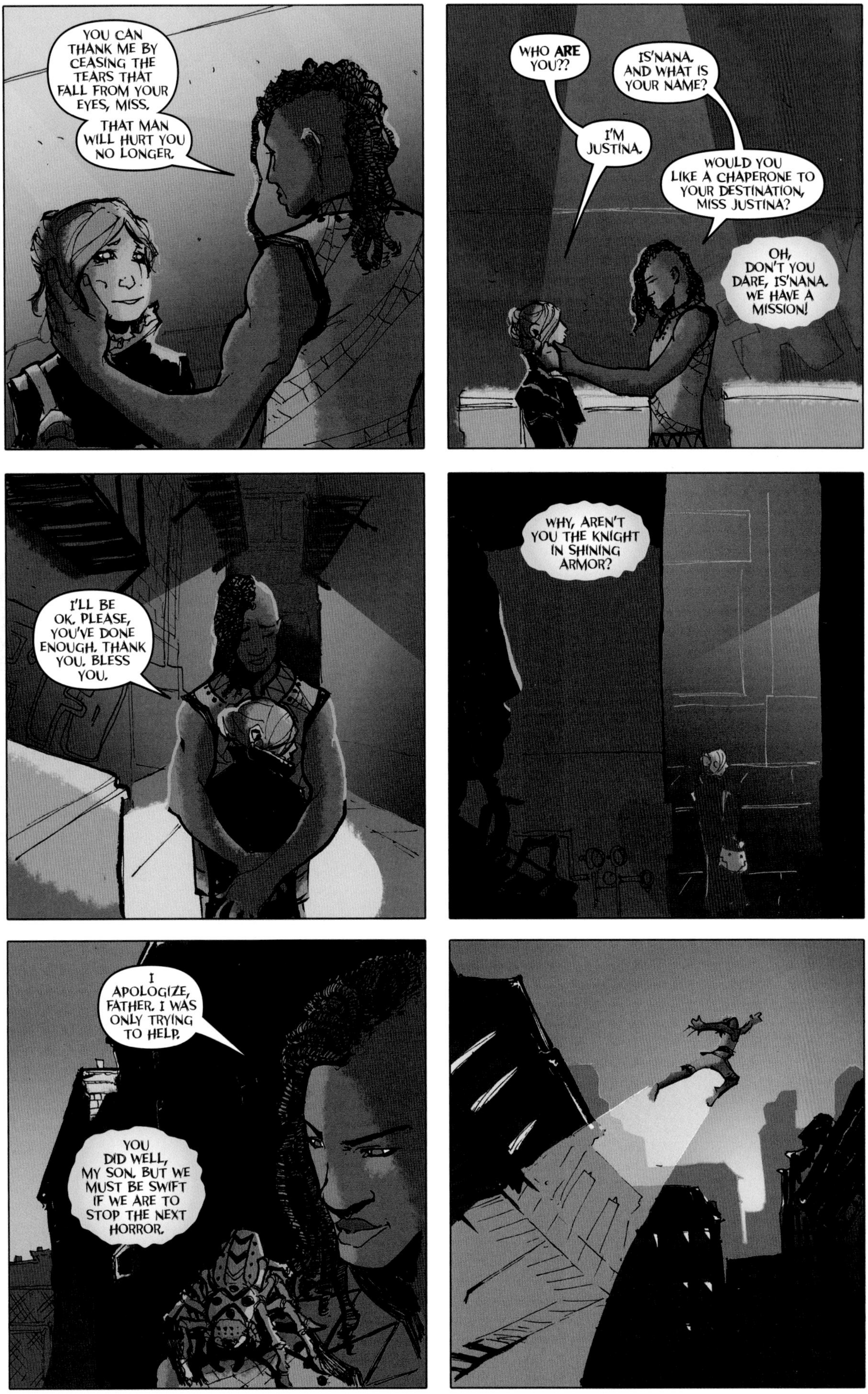
YOU CAN THANK ME BY CEASING THE TEARS THAT FALL FROM YOUR EYES, MISS.
THAT MAN WILL HURT YOU NO LONGER.
WHO ARE YOU??
IS'NANA. AND WHAT IS YOUR NAME?
I'M JUSTINA.
WOULD YOU LIKE A CHAPERONE TO YOUR DESTINATION, MISS JUSTINA?
OH, DON'T YOU DARE, IS'NANA. WE HAVE A MISSION!
I'LL BE OK. PLEASE, YOU'VE DONE ENOUGH. THANK YOU. BLESS YOU.
WHY, AREN'T YOU THE KNIGHT IN SHINING ARMOR?
I APOLOGIZE, FATHER. I WAS ONLY TRYING TO HELP.
YOU DID WELL, MY SON. BUT WE MUST BE SWIFT IF WE ARE TO STOP THE NEXT HORROR.

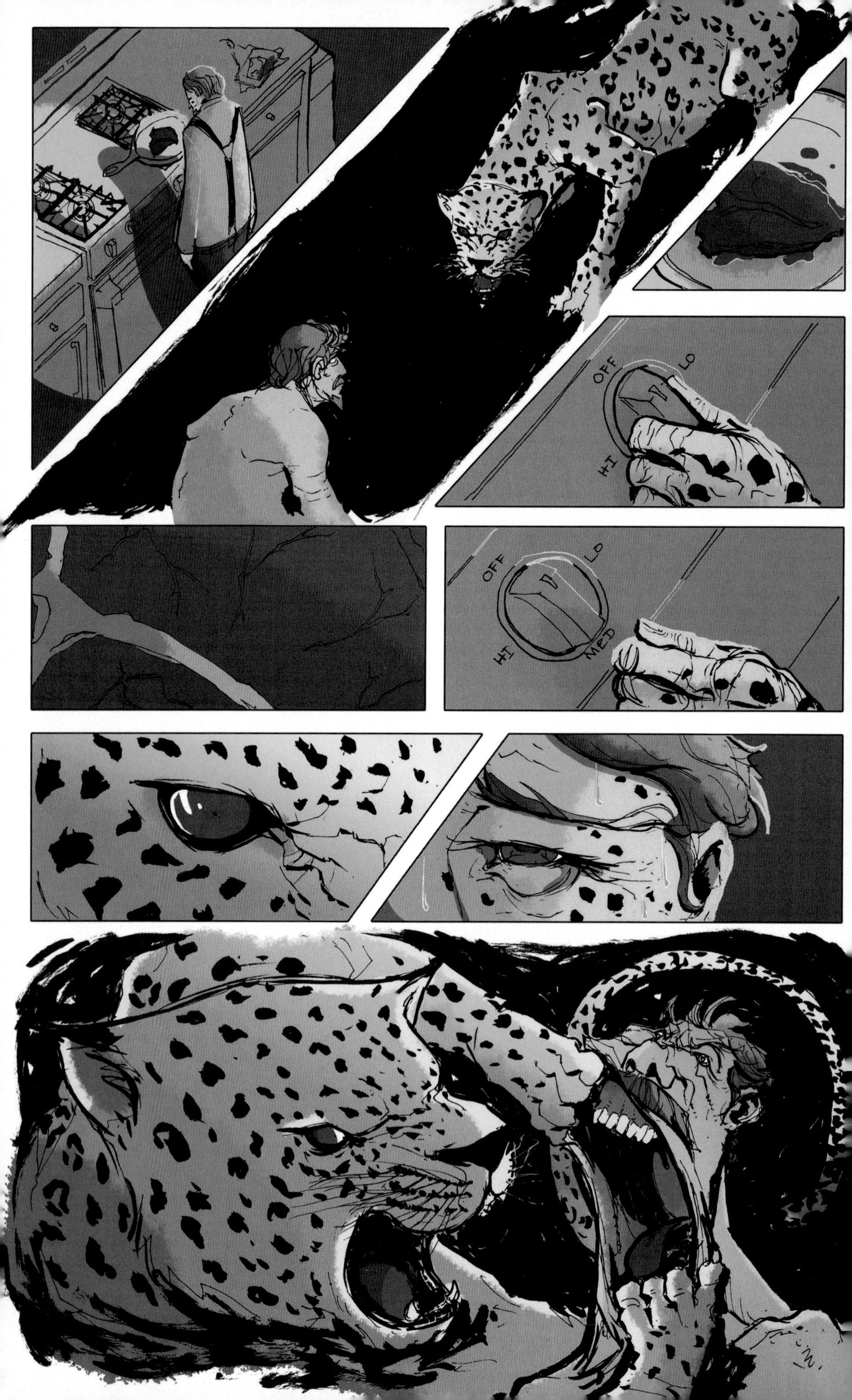
OFF
LO
HI
OFF
LO
MED
HI

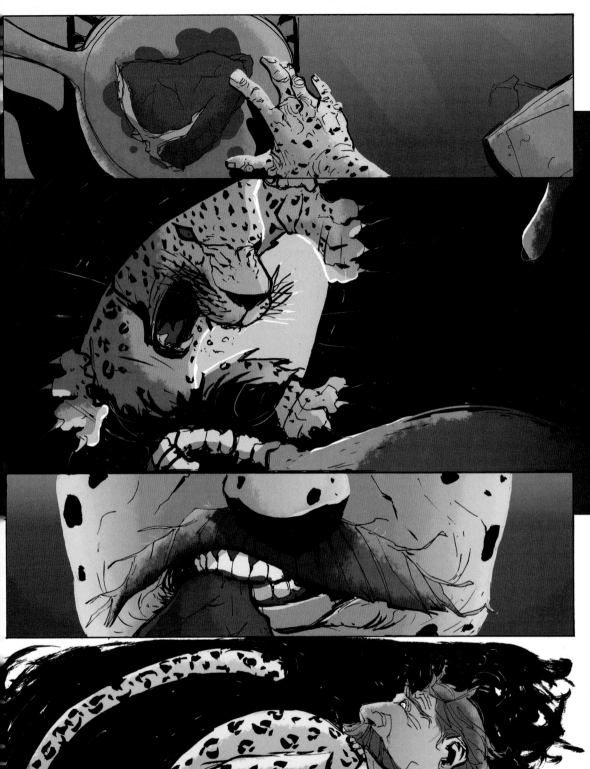

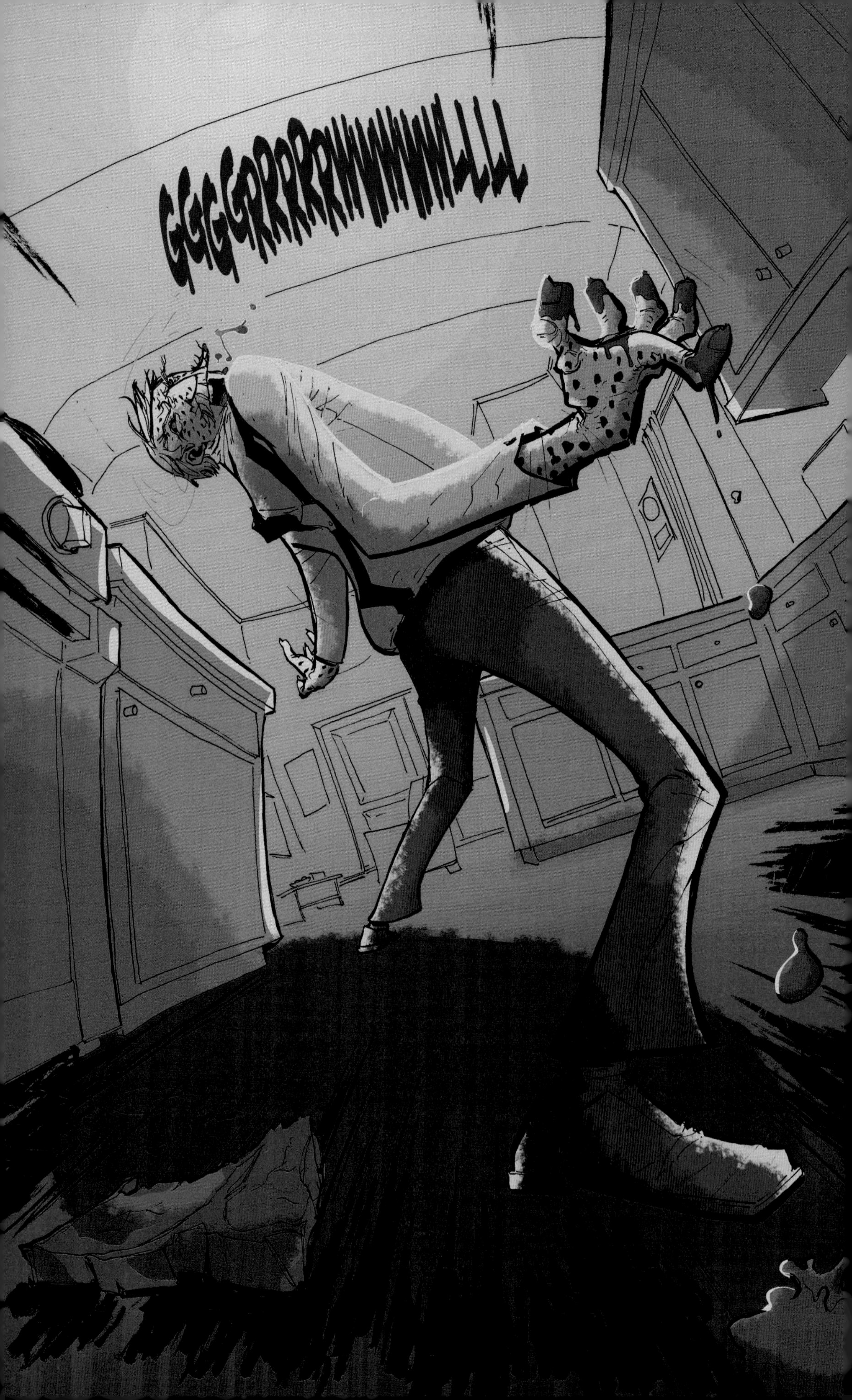
GGGGRRRRWWWWWLLLL

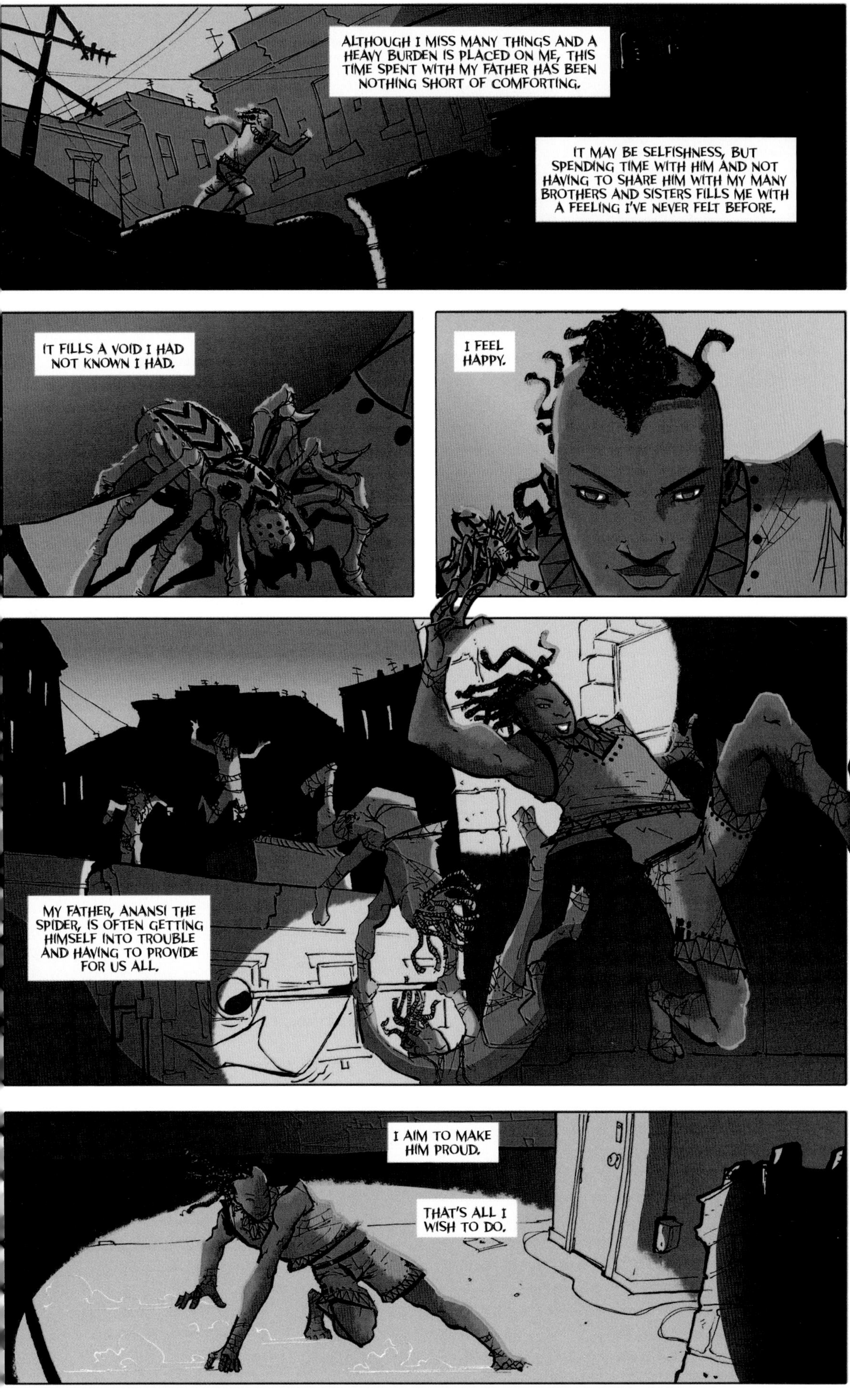
ALTHOUGH I MISS MANY THINGS AND A HEAVY BURDEN IS PLACED ON ME, THIS TIME SPENT WITH MY FATHER HAS BEEN NOTHING SHORT OF COMFORTING.
IT MAY BE SELFISHNESS, BUT SPENDING TIME WITH HIM AND NOT HAVING TO SHARE HIM WITH MY MANY BROTHERS AND SISTERS FILLS ME WITH A FEELING I'VE NEVER FELT BEFORE.
IT FILLS A VOID I HAD NOT KNOWN I HAD.
I FEEL HAPPY.
MY FATHER, ANANSI THE SPIDER, IS OFTEN GETTING HIMSELF INTO TROUBLE AND HAVING TO PROVIDE FOR US ALL.
I AIM TO MAKE HIM PROUD.
THAT'S ALL I WISH TO DO.

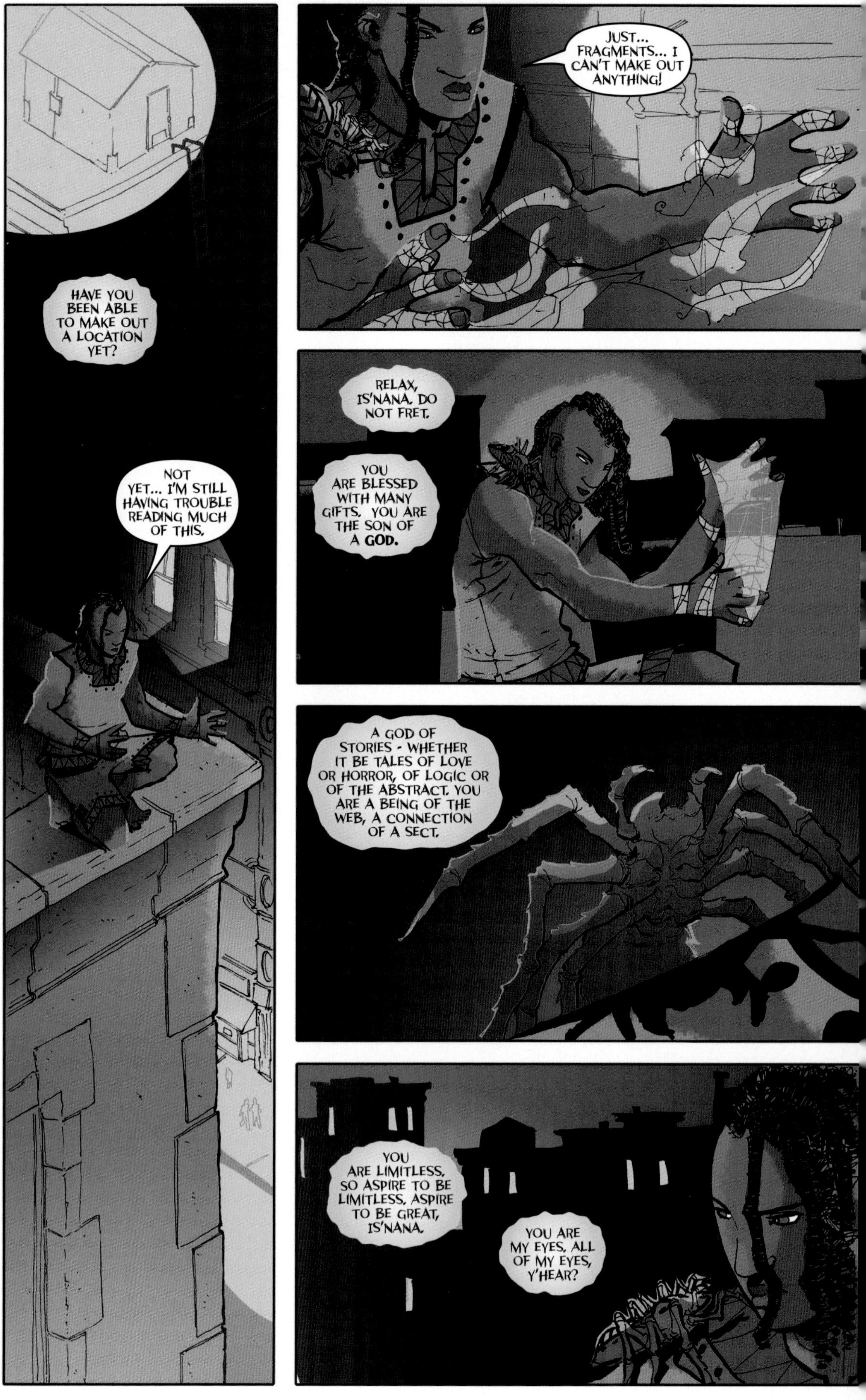
HAVE YOU BEEN ABLE TO MAKE OUT A LOCATION YET?
NOT YET... I'M STILL HAVING TROUBLE READING MUCH OF THIS.
JUST... FRAGMENTS... I CAN'T MAKE OUT ANYTHING!
RELAX, IS'NANA. DO NOT FRET.
YOU ARE BLESSED WITH MANY GIFTS. YOU ARE THE SON OF A **GOD.**
A GOD OF STORIES - WHETHER IT BE TALES OF LOVE OR HORROR, OF LOGIC OR OF THE ABSTRACT. YOU ARE A BEING OF THE WEB, A CONNECTION OF A SECT.
YOU ARE LIMITLESS, SO ASPIRE TO BE LIMITLESS. ASPIRE TO BE GREAT, IS'NANA.
YOU ARE MY EYES, ALL OF MY EYES, Y'HEAR?

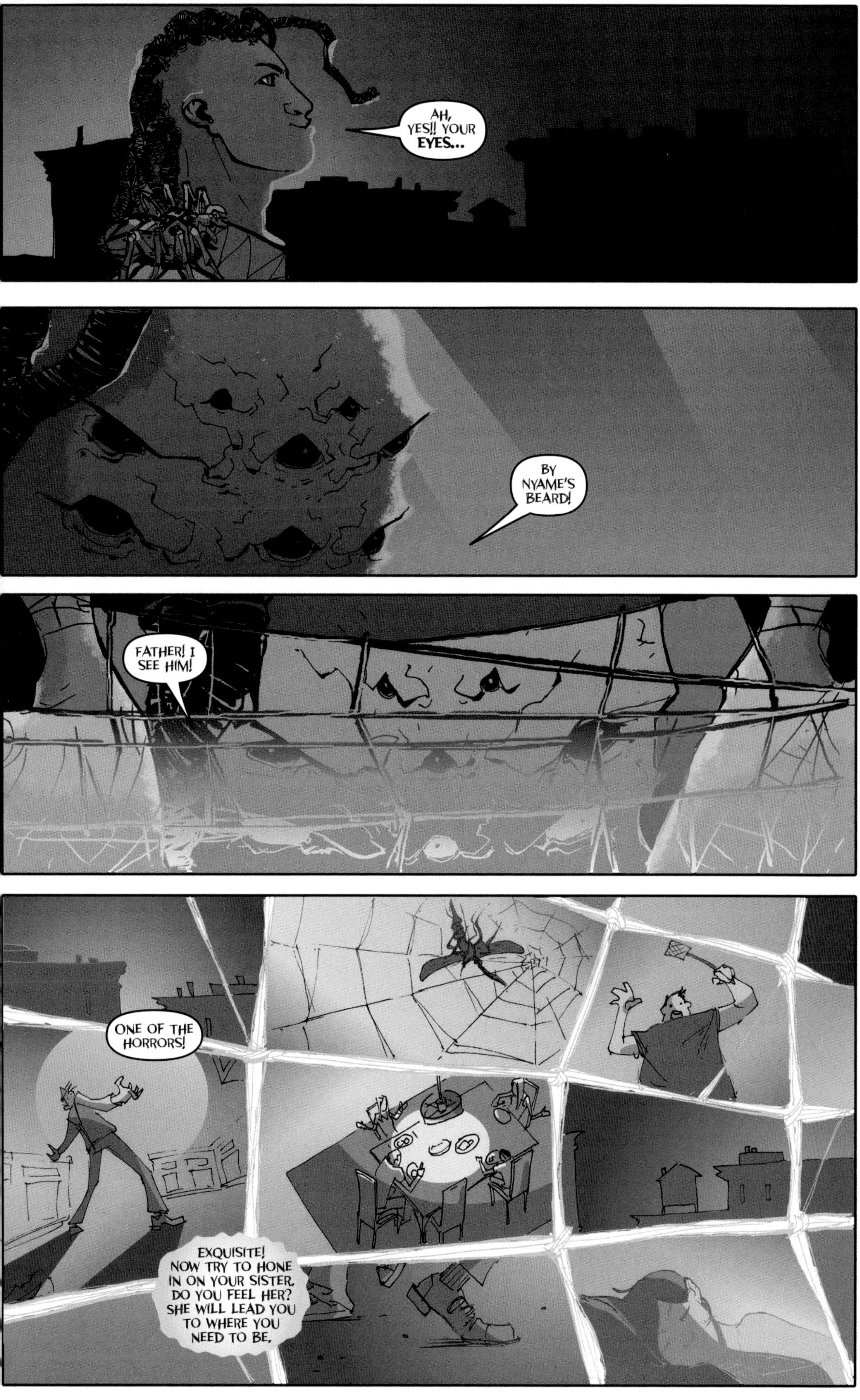
AH, YES!! YOUR EYES...
BY NYAME'S BEARD!
FATHER! I SEE HIM!
ONE OF THE HORRORS!
EXQUISITE! NOW TRY TO HONE IN ON YOUR SISTER. DO YOU FEEL HER? SHE WILL LEAD YOU TO WHERE YOU NEED TO BE.

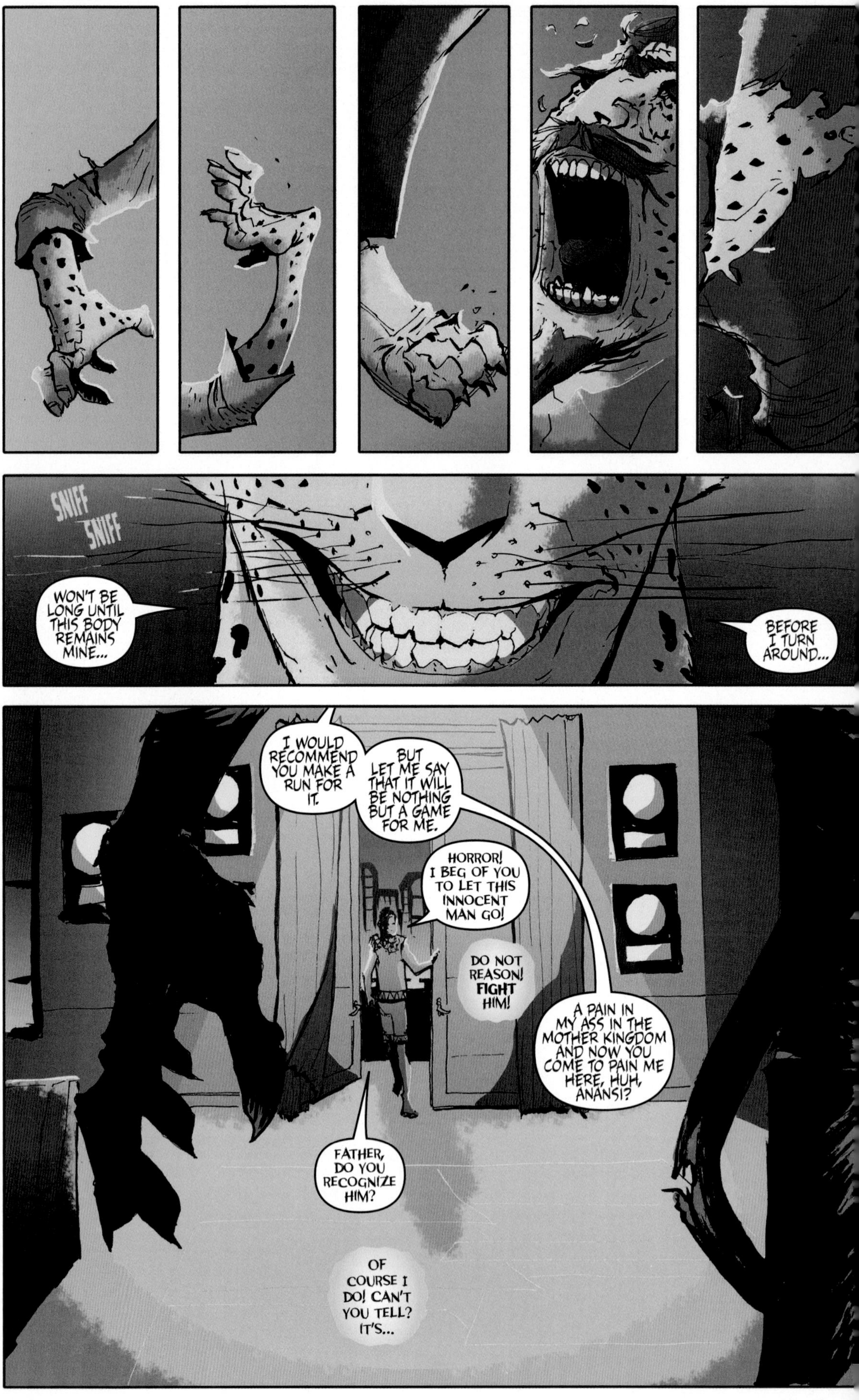
SNIFF
SNIFF
WON'T BE LONG UNTIL THIS BODY REMAINS MINE...
BEFORE I TURN AROUND...
I WOULD RECOMMEND YOU MAKE A RUN FOR IT.
BUT LET ME SAY THAT IT WILL BE NOTHING BUT A GAME FOR ME.
HORROR! I BEG OF YOU TO LET THIS INNOCENT MAN GO!
DO NOT REASON! **FIGHT** HIM!
A PAIN IN MY ASS IN THE MOTHER KINGDOM AND NOW YOU COME TO PAIN ME HERE, HUH, ANANSI?
FATHER, DO YOU RECOGNIZE HIM?
OF COURSE I DO! CAN'T YOU TELL? IT'S...

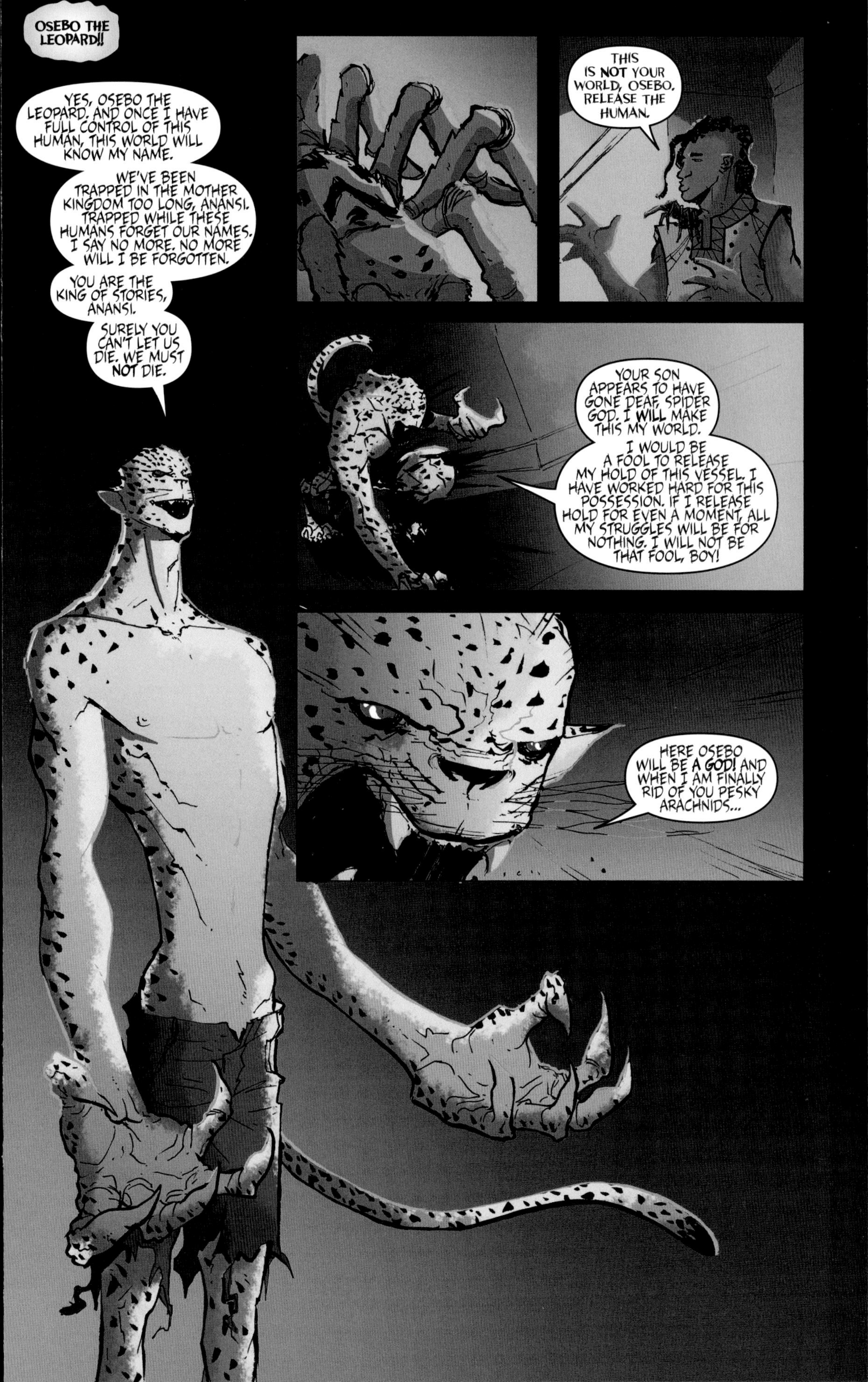

OSEBO THE LEOPARD!!
YES, OSEBO THE LEOPARD. AND ONCE I HAVE FULL CONTROL OF THIS HUMAN, THIS WORLD WILL KNOW MY NAME.
WE'VE BEEN TRAPPED IN THE MOTHER KINGDOM TOO LONG, ANANSI. TRAPPED WHILE THESE HUMANS FORGET OUR NAMES. I SAY NO MORE. NO MORE WILL I BE FORGOTTEN.
YOU ARE THE KING OF STORIES, ANANSI.
SURELY YOU CAN'T LET US DIE. WE MUST **NOT** DIE.
THIS IS **NOT** YOUR WORLD, OSEBO. RELEASE THE HUMAN.
YOUR SON APPEARS TO HAVE GONE DEAF, SPIDER GOD. I **WILL** MAKE THIS MY WORLD.
I WOULD BE A FOOL TO RELEASE MY HOLD OF THIS VESSEL. I HAVE WORKED HARD FOR THIS POSSESSION. IF I RELEASE HOLD FOR EVEN A MOMENT, ALL MY STRUGGLES WILL BE FOR NOTHING. I WILL NOT BE THAT FOOL, BOY!
HERE OSEBO WILL BE **A GOD!** AND WHEN I AM FINALLY RID OF YOU PESKY ARACHNIDS...

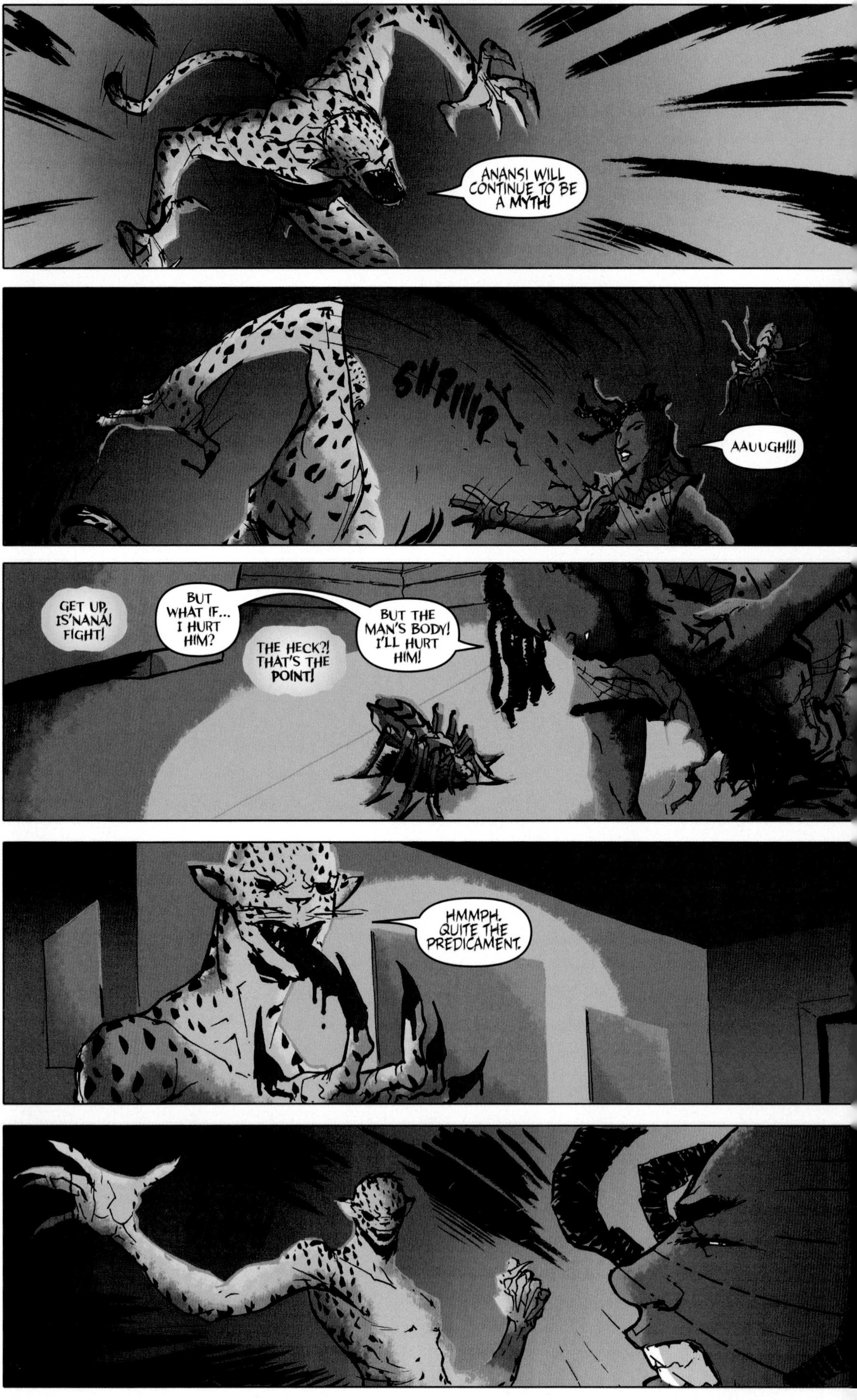
ANANSI WILL CONTINUE TO BE A MYTH!
SHRIIIP
AAUUGH!!!
GET UP, IS'NANA! FIGHT!
BUT WHAT IF... I HURT HIM?
THE HECK?! THAT'S THE POINT!
BUT THE MAN'S BODY! I'LL HURT HIM!
HMMPH. QUITE THE PREDICAMENT.

OH NYAME'S BEARD! IS'NANA, THE MAN IS GONE! HE IS GONE! IF YOU DON'T STOP OSEBO, IT'LL ONLY END IN MORE MISERY.

IS THERE NO OTHER WAY?

OF COURSE LEAVE IT TO YOU - OF ALL MY CHILDREN - TO BE THE PACIFIST.

OSEBO, PLEASE, I BEG OF YOU.

NO! DON'T BEG! ESPECIALLY NOT TO OSEBO!

THIS MAN SHOULDN'T BE A PART OF THIS. HE MAY HAVE A FAMILY TO CARE FOR.

CHILDREN, HAVE YOU NO HEART?

I GROW TIRED OF YOUR GROVELING.

GROWL

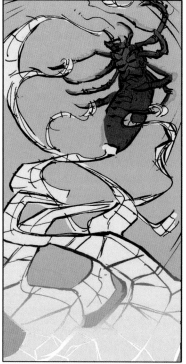

GAH!!!

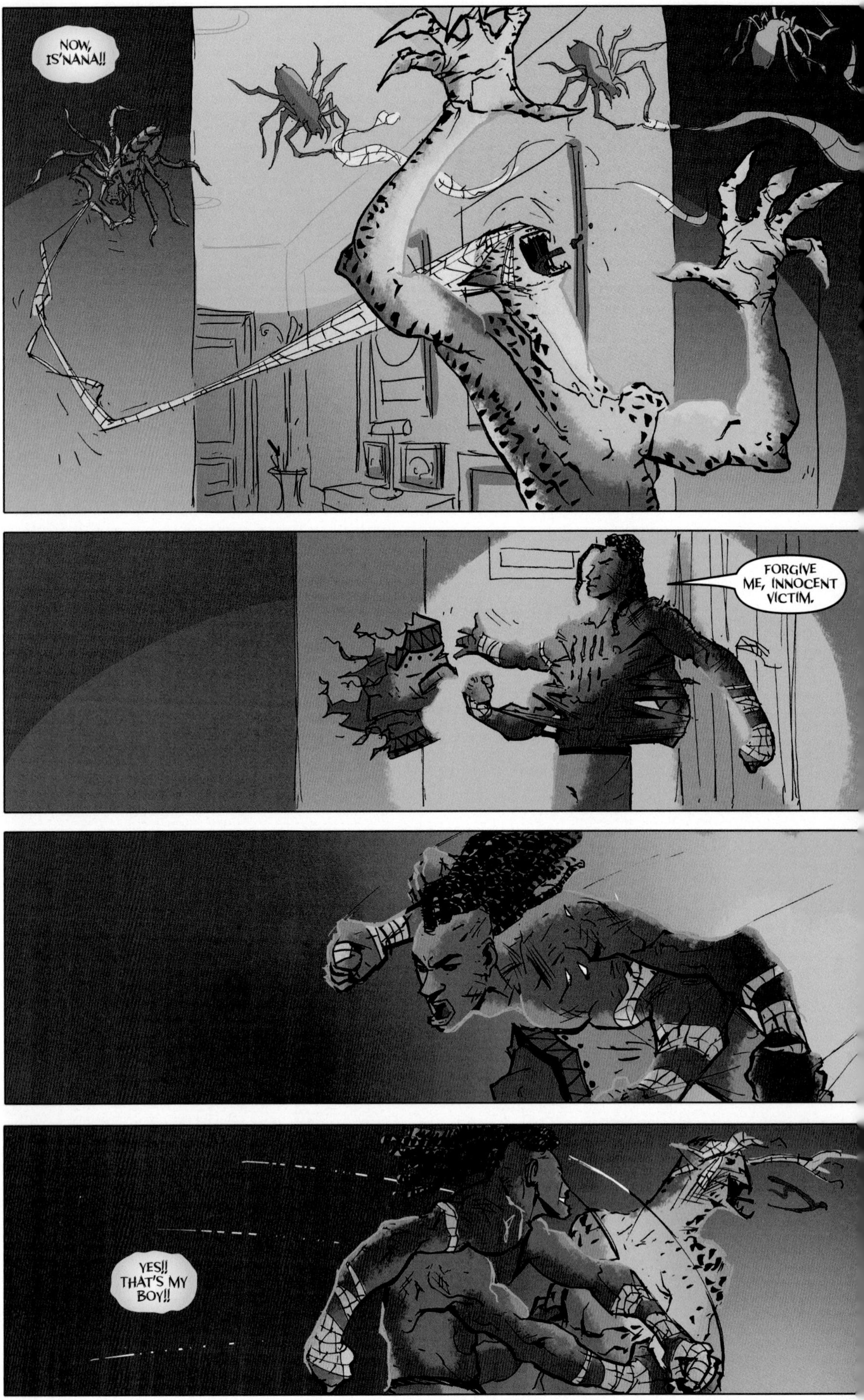
NOW, IS'NANA!!
FORGIVE ME, INNOCENT VICTIM.
YES!! THAT'S MY BOY!!

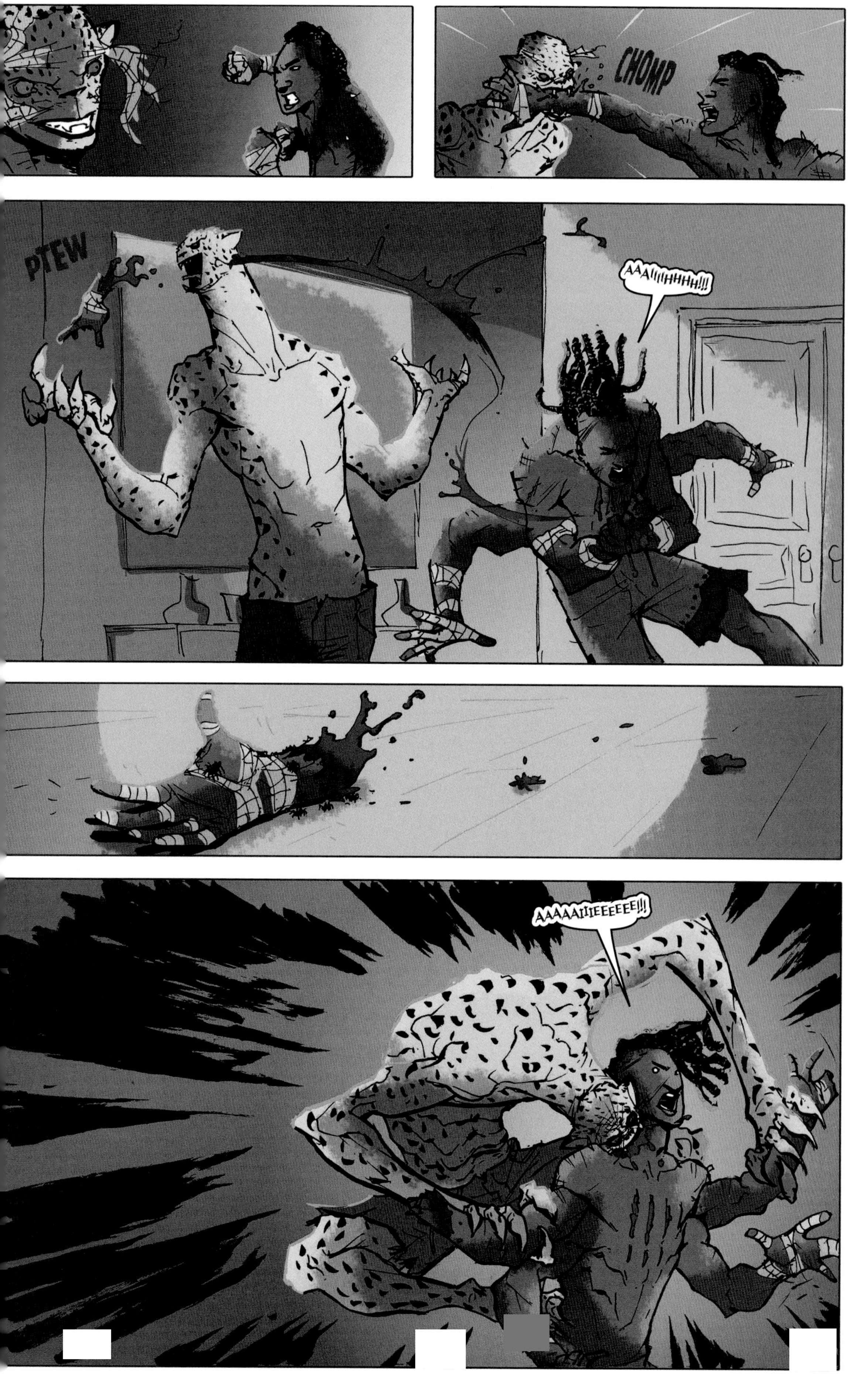
CHOMP
PTEW
AAAIIIIHHHHH!!!
AAAAAIIIIEEEEEEE!!!

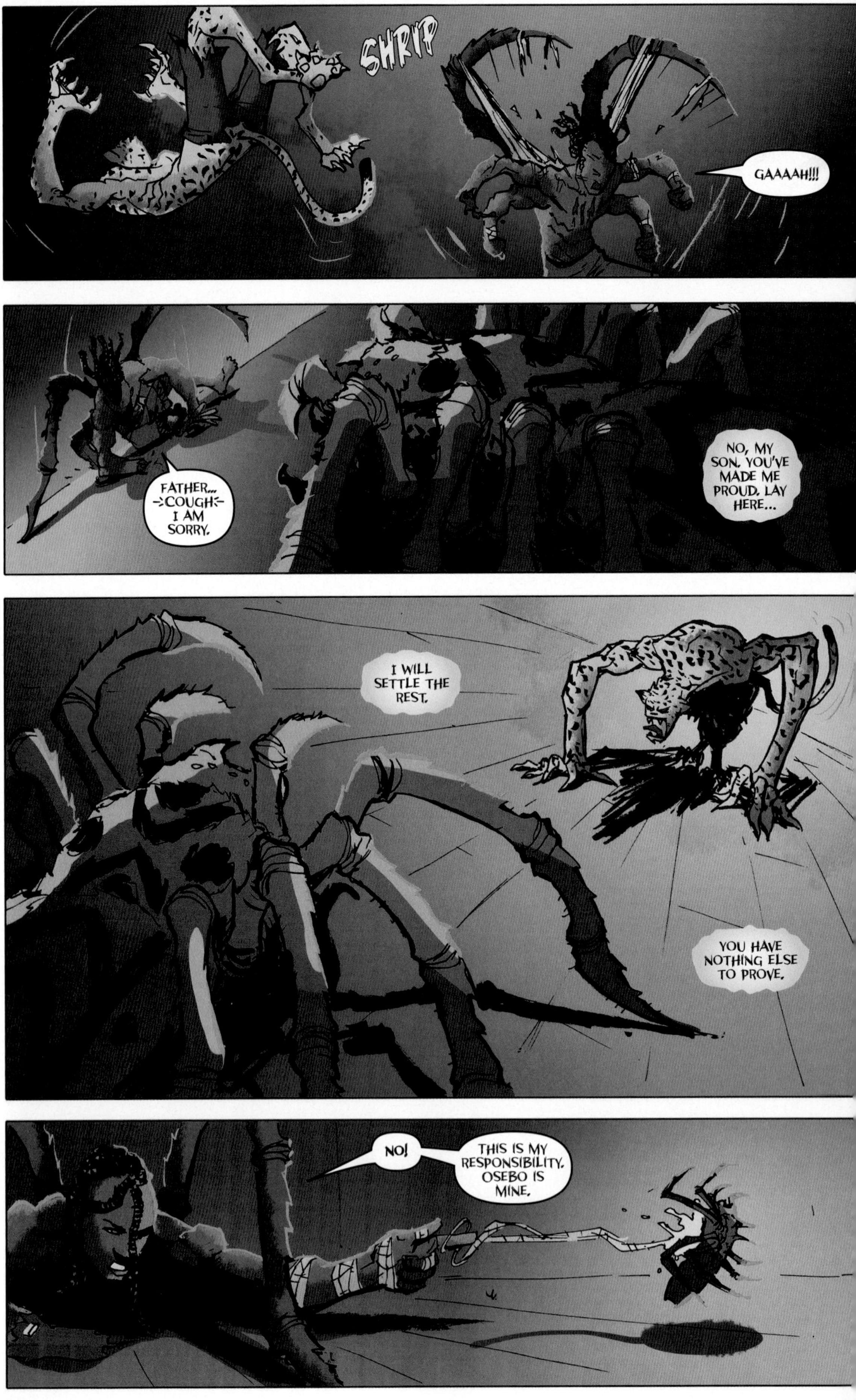
SHRIP
GAAAAH!!!
FATHER... -COUGH- I AM SORRY.
NO, MY SON. YOU'VE MADE ME PROUD. LAY HERE...
I WILL SETTLE THE REST.
YOU HAVE NOTHING ELSE TO PROVE.
NO!
THIS IS MY RESPONSIBILITY. OSEBO IS MINE.

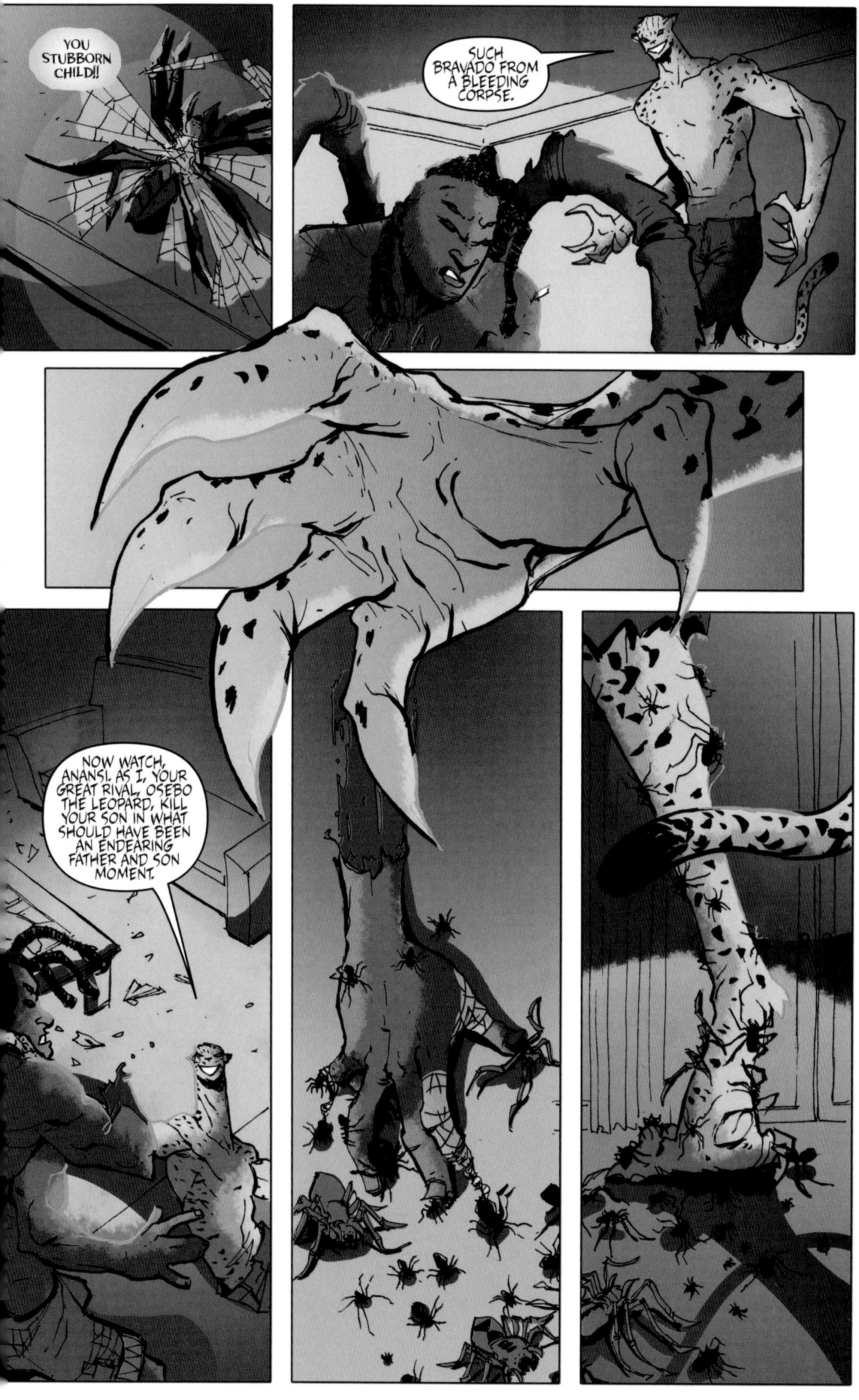
YOU STUBBORN CHILD!!
SUCH BRAVADO FROM A BLEEDING CORPSE.
NOW WATCH, ANANSI. AS I, YOUR GREAT RIVAL, OSEBO THE LEOPARD, KILL YOUR SON IN WHAT SHOULD HAVE BEEN AN ENDEARING FATHER AND SON MOMENT.

WHAT IS THIS?

I AM LIMITLESS, I AM MANY, A LEGION OF THE ARACHNID. I AM MY FATHER'S SON, I AM IS'NANA! AND YOU WILL KNOW MY NAME AS THE SOUND OF YOUR DEFEAT, OSEBO!

WHAT... WHAT DID YOU DO?!

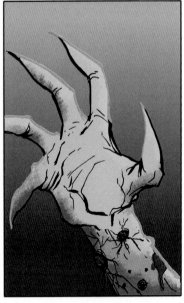

VENOM, OSEBO.

DO YOU FEEL MY POISON PIERCING THROUGH YOUR SKIN? LOOK AT IT... I MADE SURE TO UP THE INTAKE...

THAT WAY YOU CAN SEE IT, FEEL IT MOVE UP YOUR ARM AND EVENTUALLY YOUR WHOLE BODY.

NO!

ALL OF YOUR HARD WORK WILL BE FOR NOTHING.

YOU WILL DIE IN THIS BODY.

NO! HOW DARE YOU!?

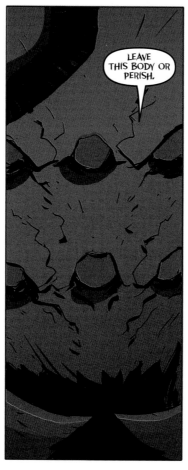

LEAVE THIS BODY OR PERISH.

YOU FILTH! YOU WILL GET YOURS, BOY! I WILL NOT LEAVE THIS BODY!

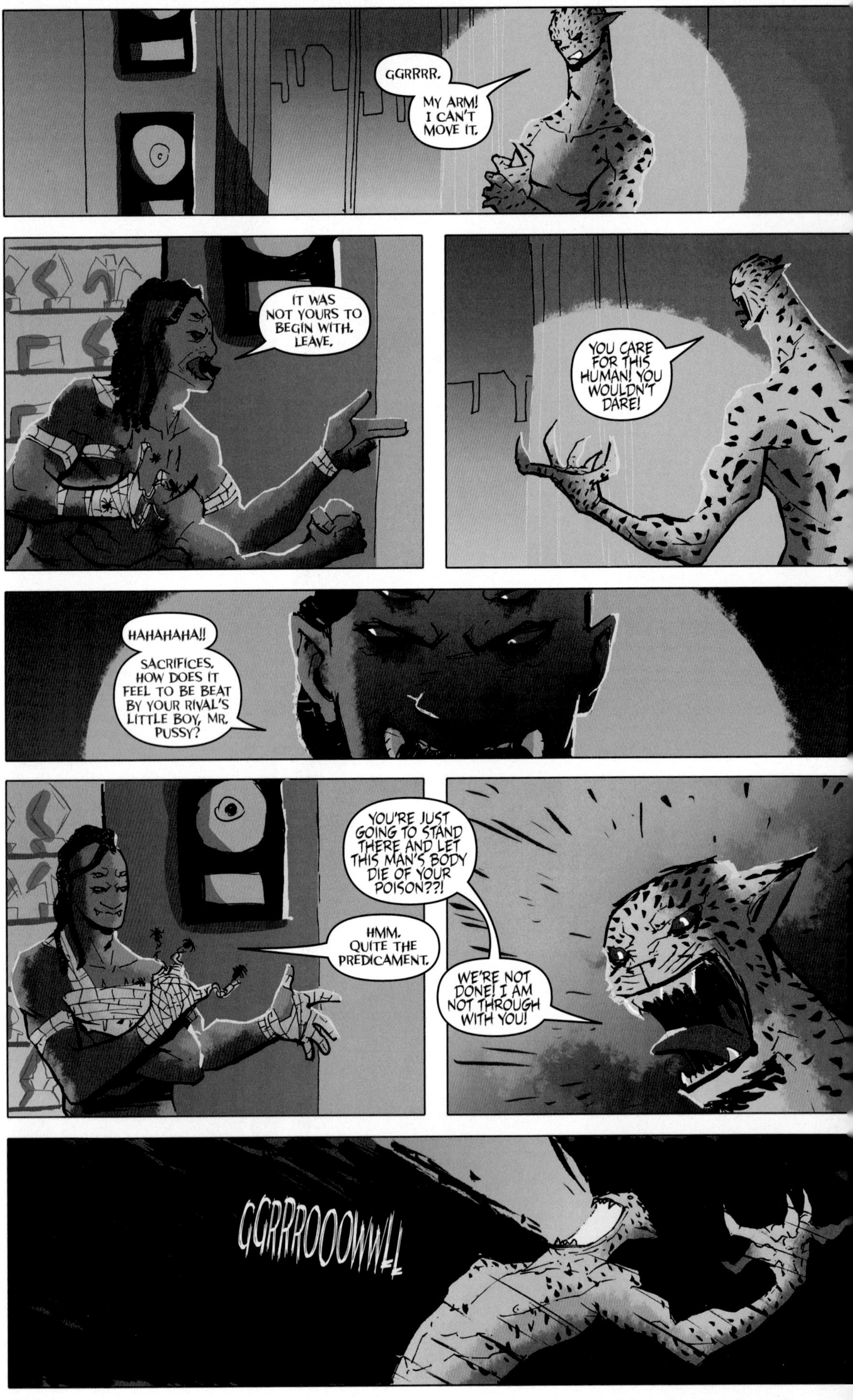
GGRRRR.
MY ARM! I CAN'T MOVE IT.
IT WAS NOT YOURS TO BEGIN WITH. LEAVE.
YOU CARE FOR THIS HUMAN! YOU WOULDN'T DARE!
HAHAHAHA!!
SACRIFICES. HOW DOES IT FEEL TO BE BEAT BY YOUR RIVAL'S LITTLE BOY, MR. PUSSY?
YOU'RE JUST GOING TO STAND THERE AND LET THIS MAN'S BODY DIE OF YOUR POISON??!
HMM. QUITE THE PREDICAMENT.
WE'RE NOT DONE! I AM NOT THROUGH WITH YOU!
GGRRROOOWWLL

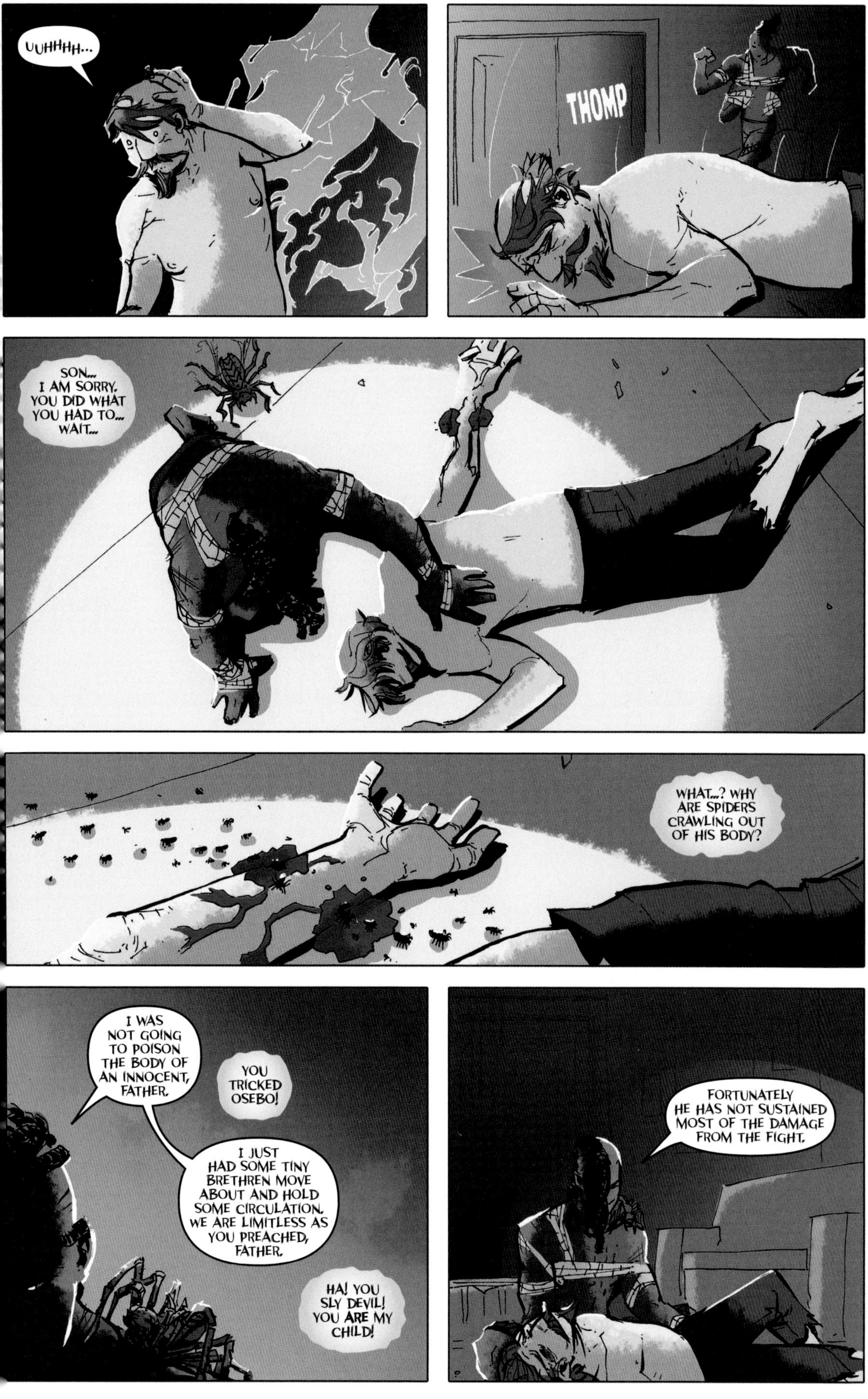
UUHHHH...
THOMP
SON... I AM SORRY. YOU DID WHAT YOU HAD TO... WAIT...
WHAT...? WHY ARE SPIDERS CRAWLING OUT OF HIS BODY?
I WAS NOT GOING TO POISON THE BODY OF AN INNOCENT, FATHER.
YOU TRICKED OSEBO!
I JUST HAD SOME TINY BRETHREN MOVE ABOUT AND HOLD SOME CIRCULATION. WE ARE LIMITLESS AS YOU PREACHED, FATHER.
HA! YOU SLY DEVIL! YOU ARE MY CHILD!
FORTUNATELY HE HAS NOT SUSTAINED MOST OF THE DAMAGE FROM THE FIGHT.

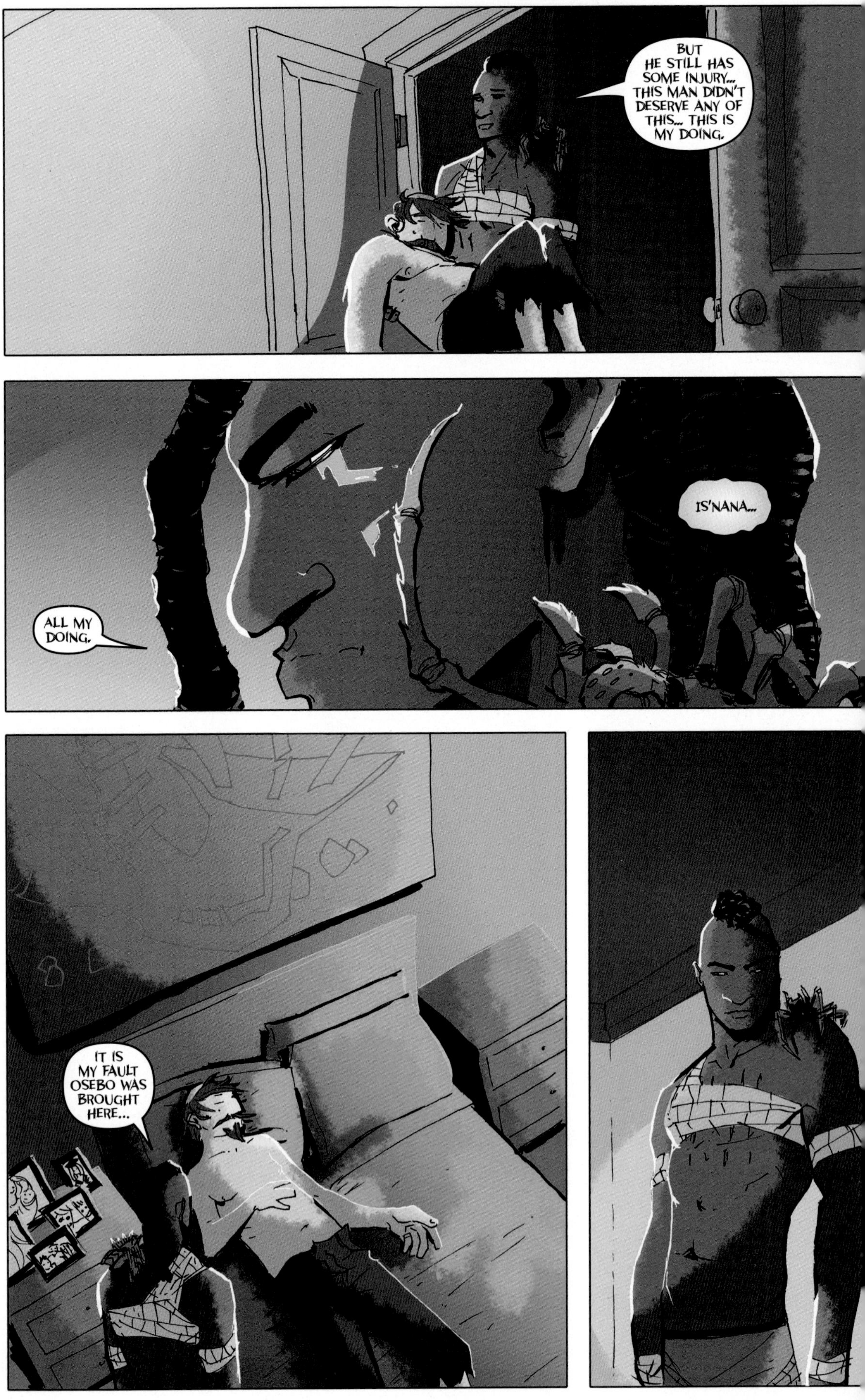
BUT HE STILL HAS SOME INJURY... THIS MAN DIDN'T DESERVE ANY OF THIS... THIS IS MY DOING.
IS'NANA...
ALL MY DOING.
IT IS MY FAULT OSEBO WAS BROUGHT HERE...

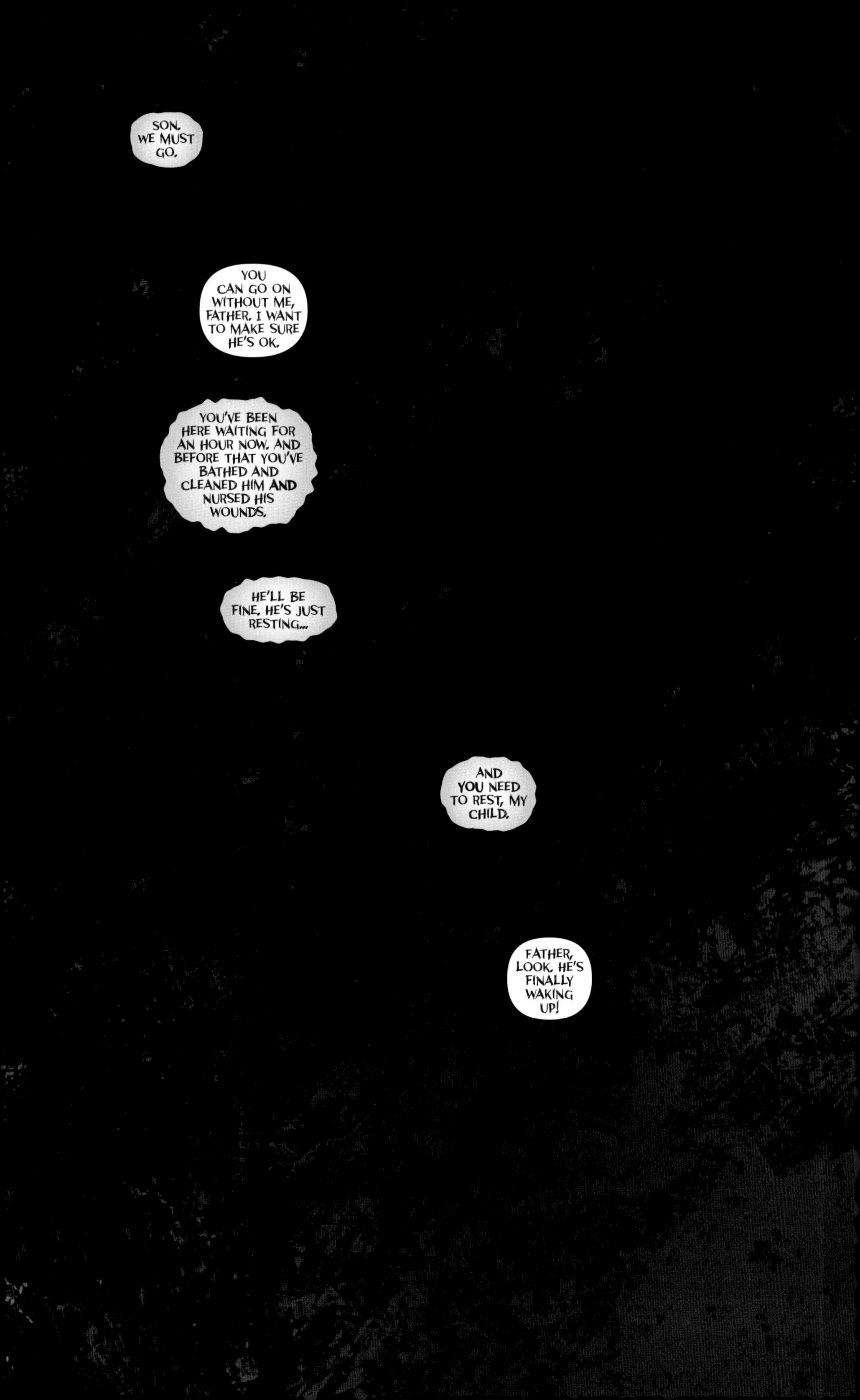
SON. WE MUST GO.
YOU CAN GO ON WITHOUT ME, FATHER. I WANT TO MAKE SURE HE'S OK.
YOU'VE BEEN HERE WAITING FOR AN HOUR NOW. AND BEFORE THAT YOU'VE BATHED AND CLEANED HIM AND NURSED HIS WOUNDS.
HE'LL BE FINE. HE'S JUST RESTING...
AND YOU NEED TO REST, MY CHILD.
FATHER, LOOK. HE'S FINALLY WAKING UP!

UH....

HEY THERE, TRY TO TAKE IT EASY. HOW ARE YOU FEELING?

YOU, I SAW YOU. YOU SAVED ME.

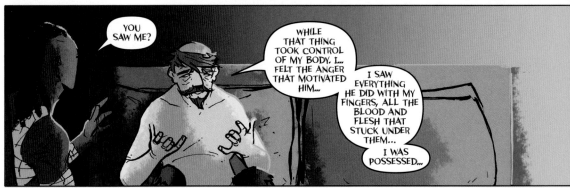

YOU SAW ME?

WHILE THAT THING TOOK CONTROL OF MY BODY. I... FELT THE ANGER THAT MOTIVATED HIM...

I SAW EVERYTHING HE DID WITH MY FINGERS, ALL THE BLOOD AND FLESH THAT STUCK UNDER THEM...

I WAS POSSESSED...

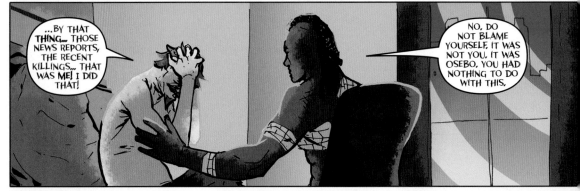

...BY THAT THING... THOSE NEWS REPORTS, THE RECENT KILLINGS... THAT WAS ME! I DID THAT!

NO, DO NOT BLAME YOURSELF. IT WAS NOT YOU. IT WAS OSEBO, YOU HAD NOTHING TO DO WITH THIS.

BUT IT WAS MY HANDS... MY MOUTH... OH GOD... HOW AM I TO LIVE WITH THIS?

THIS ISN'T SOMETHING THAT'LL GO AWAY IN HIS MIND. HIS MIND – HIS BODY – WAS VIOLATED.

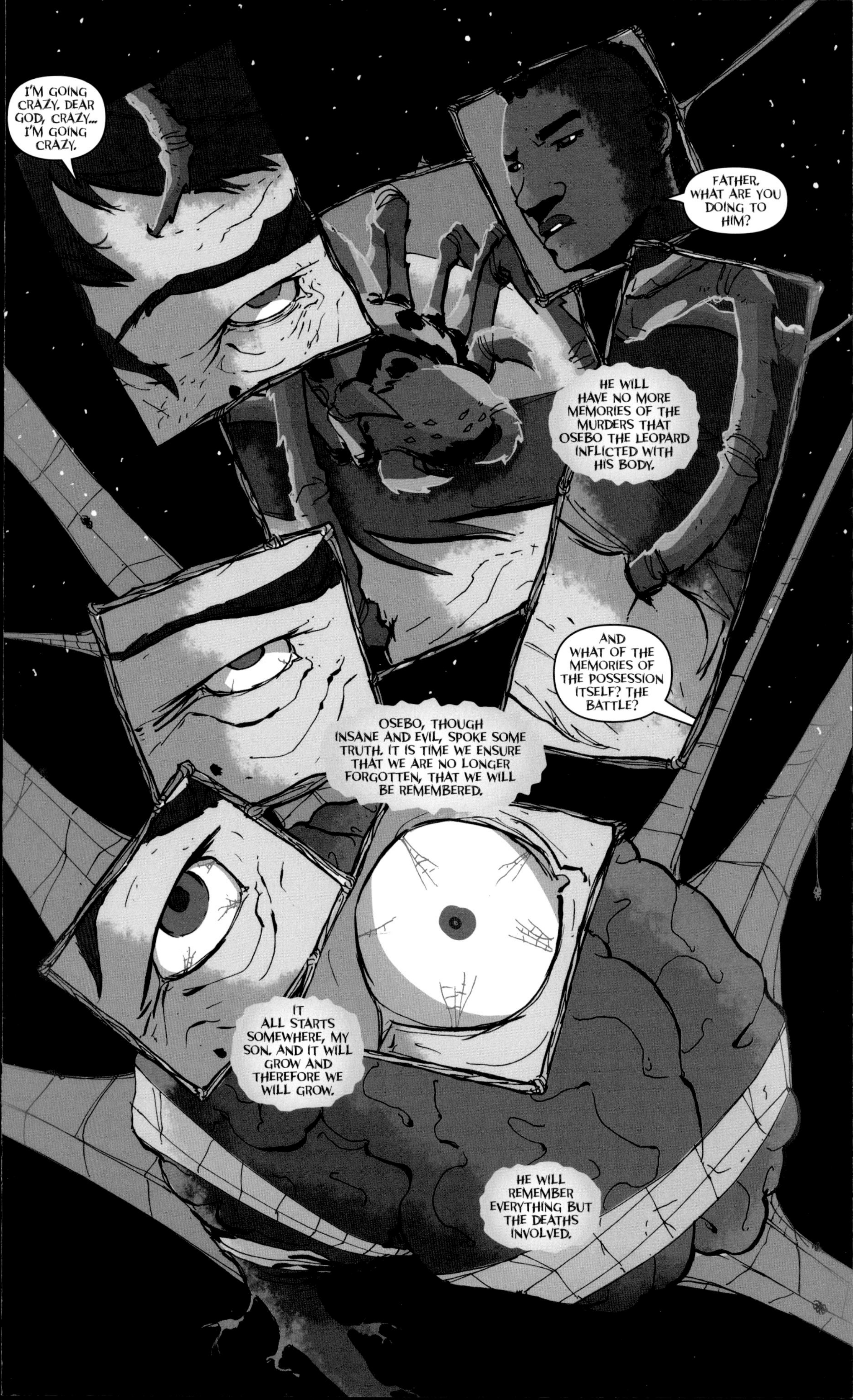
I'M GOING CRAZY. DEAR GOD, CRAZY... I'M GOING CRAZY.
FATHER. WHAT ARE YOU DOING TO HIM?
HE WILL HAVE NO MORE MEMORIES OF THE MURDERS THAT OSEBO THE LEOPARD INFLICTED WITH HIS BODY.
AND WHAT OF THE MEMORIES OF THE POSSESSION ITSELF? THE BATTLE?
OSEBO, THOUGH INSANE AND EVIL, SPOKE SOME TRUTH. IT IS TIME WE ENSURE THAT WE ARE NO LONGER FORGOTTEN, THAT WE WILL BE REMEMBERED.
IT ALL STARTS SOMEWHERE, MY SON. AND IT WILL GROW AND THEREFORE WE WILL GROW.
HE WILL REMEMBER EVERYTHING BUT THE DEATHS INVOLVED.

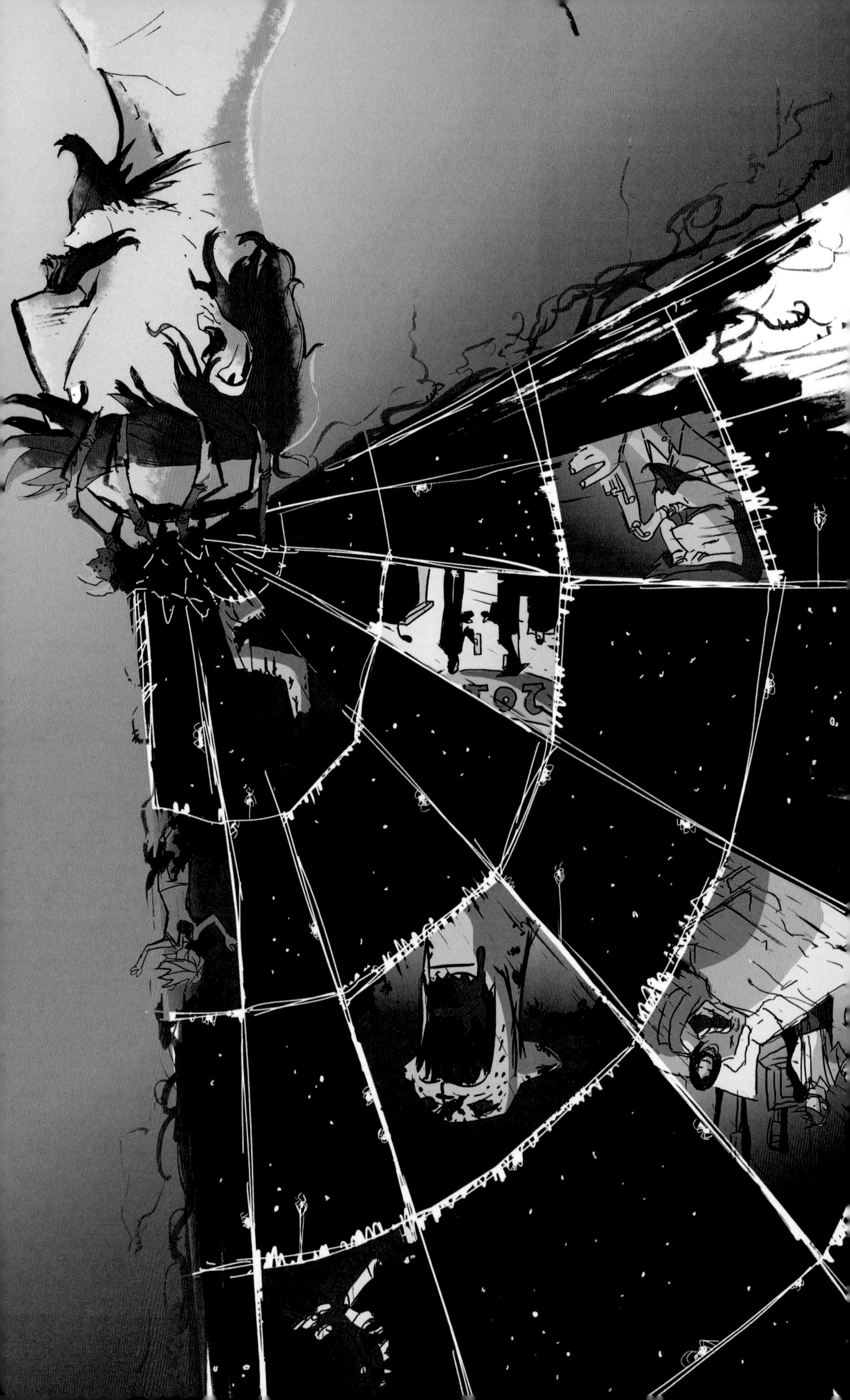

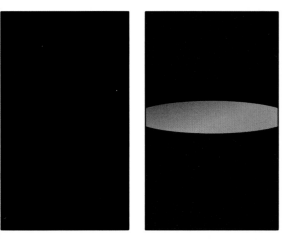

UH... MY HEAD...

EASY NOW. YOU'RE OK.

YOU, I SAW YOU. YOU SAVED ME.

...

WHILE THAT... THING TOOK CONTROL OF MY BODY...

OH, GOD... I...

...WHAT HE MADE ME DO TO YOU...

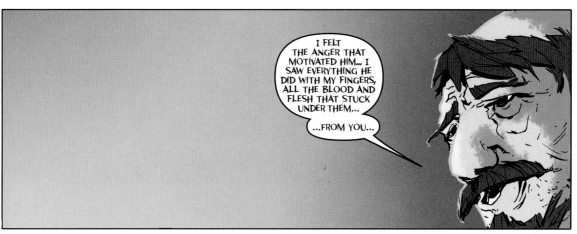

I FELT THE ANGER THAT MOTIVATED HIM... I SAW EVERYTHING HE DID WITH MY FINGERS, ALL THE BLOOD AND FLESH THAT STUCK UNDER THEM...

...FROM YOU...

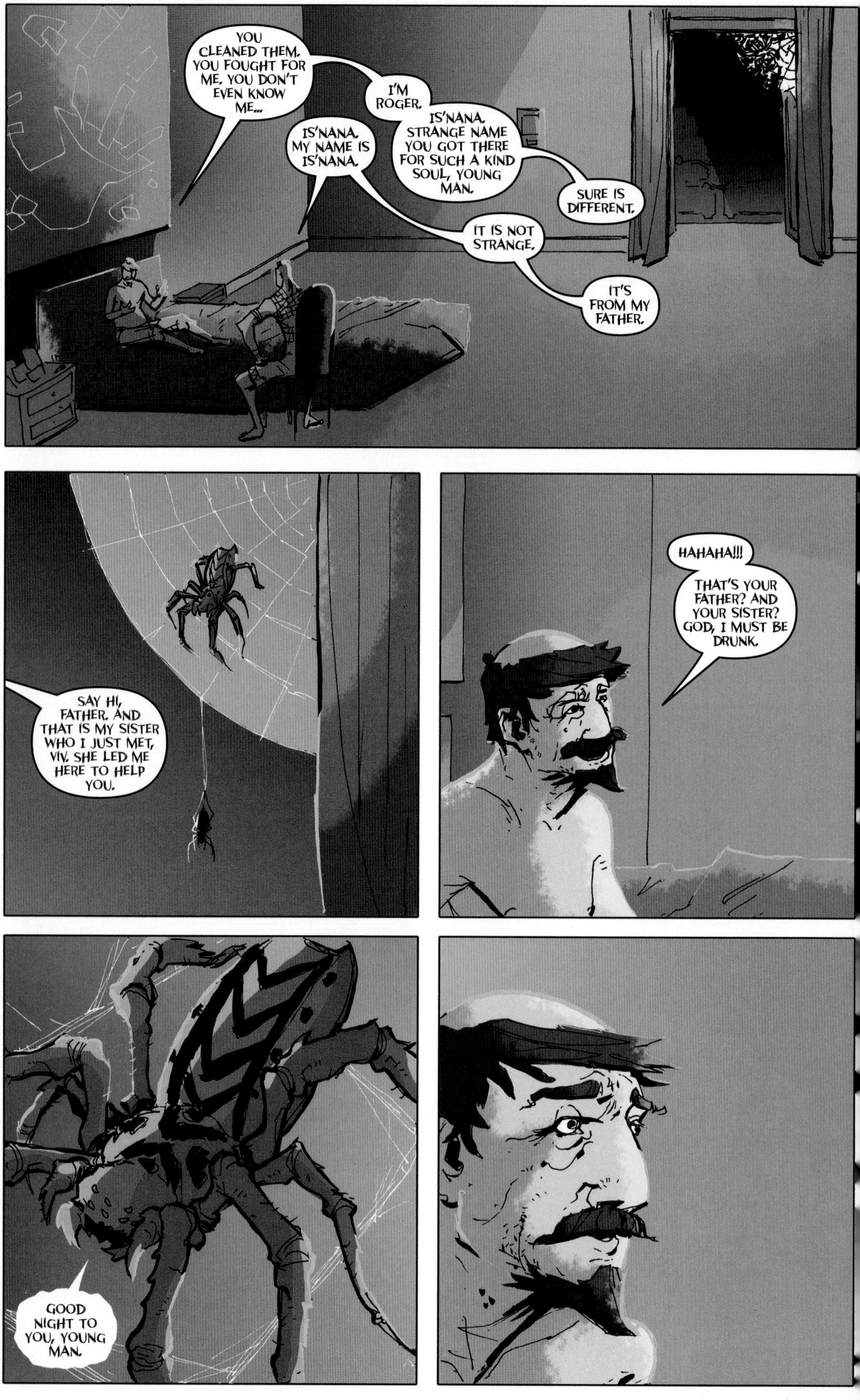
YOU CLEANED THEM. YOU FOUGHT FOR ME. YOU DON'T EVEN KNOW ME...
I'M ROGER.
IS'NANA. MY NAME IS IS'NANA.
IS'NANA. STRANGE NAME YOU GOT THERE FOR SUCH A KIND SOUL, YOUNG MAN.
SURE IS DIFFERENT.
IT IS NOT STRANGE.
IT'S FROM MY FATHER.
SAY HI, FATHER. AND THAT IS MY SISTER WHO I JUST MET, VIV. SHE LED ME HERE TO HELP YOU.
HAHAHA!!!
THAT'S YOUR FATHER? AND YOUR SISTER? GOD, I MUST BE DRUNK.
GOOD NIGHT TO YOU, YOUNG MAN.

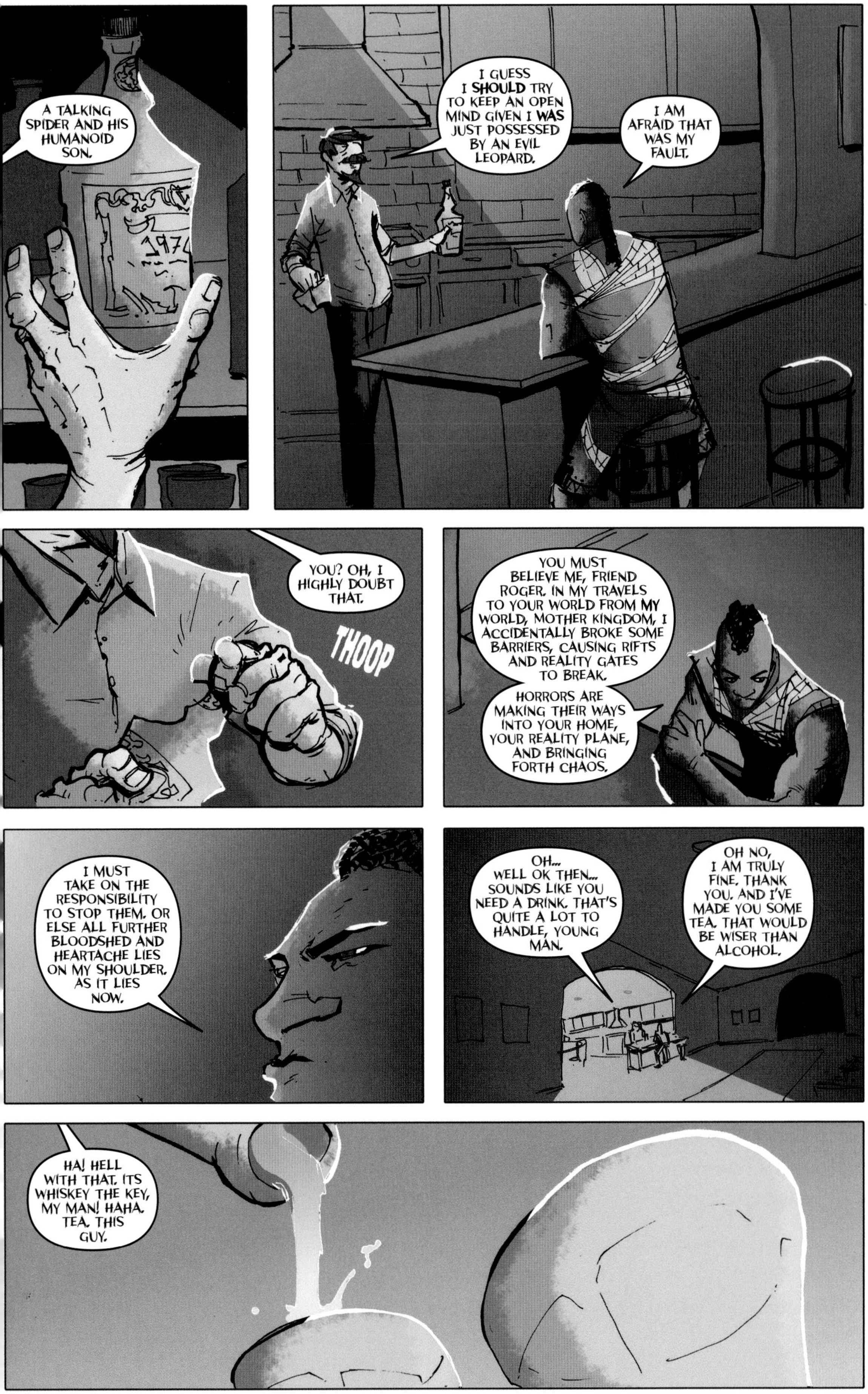

A TALKING SPIDER AND HIS HUMANOID SON.
I GUESS I SHOULD TRY TO KEEP AN OPEN MIND GIVEN I WAS JUST POSSESSED BY AN EVIL LEOPARD.
I AM AFRAID THAT WAS MY FAULT.
YOU? OH, I HIGHLY DOUBT THAT.
THOOP
YOU MUST BELIEVE ME, FRIEND ROGER. IN MY TRAVELS TO YOUR WORLD FROM MY WORLD, MOTHER KINGDOM, I ACCIDENTALLY BROKE SOME BARRIERS, CAUSING RIFTS AND REALITY GATES TO BREAK.
HORRORS ARE MAKING THEIR WAYS INTO YOUR HOME, YOUR REALITY PLANE, AND BRINGING FORTH CHAOS.
I MUST TAKE ON THE RESPONSIBILITY TO STOP THEM. OR ELSE ALL FURTHER BLOODSHED AND HEARTACHE LIES ON MY SHOULDER. AS IT LIES NOW.
OH... WELL OK THEN... SOUNDS LIKE YOU NEED A DRINK. THAT'S QUITE A LOT TO HANDLE, YOUNG MAN.
OH NO, I AM TRULY FINE. THANK YOU. AND I'VE MADE YOU SOME TEA. THAT WOULD BE WISER THAN ALCOHOL.
HA! HELL WITH THAT. ITS WHISKEY THE KEY, MY MAN! HAHA. TEA. THIS GUY.

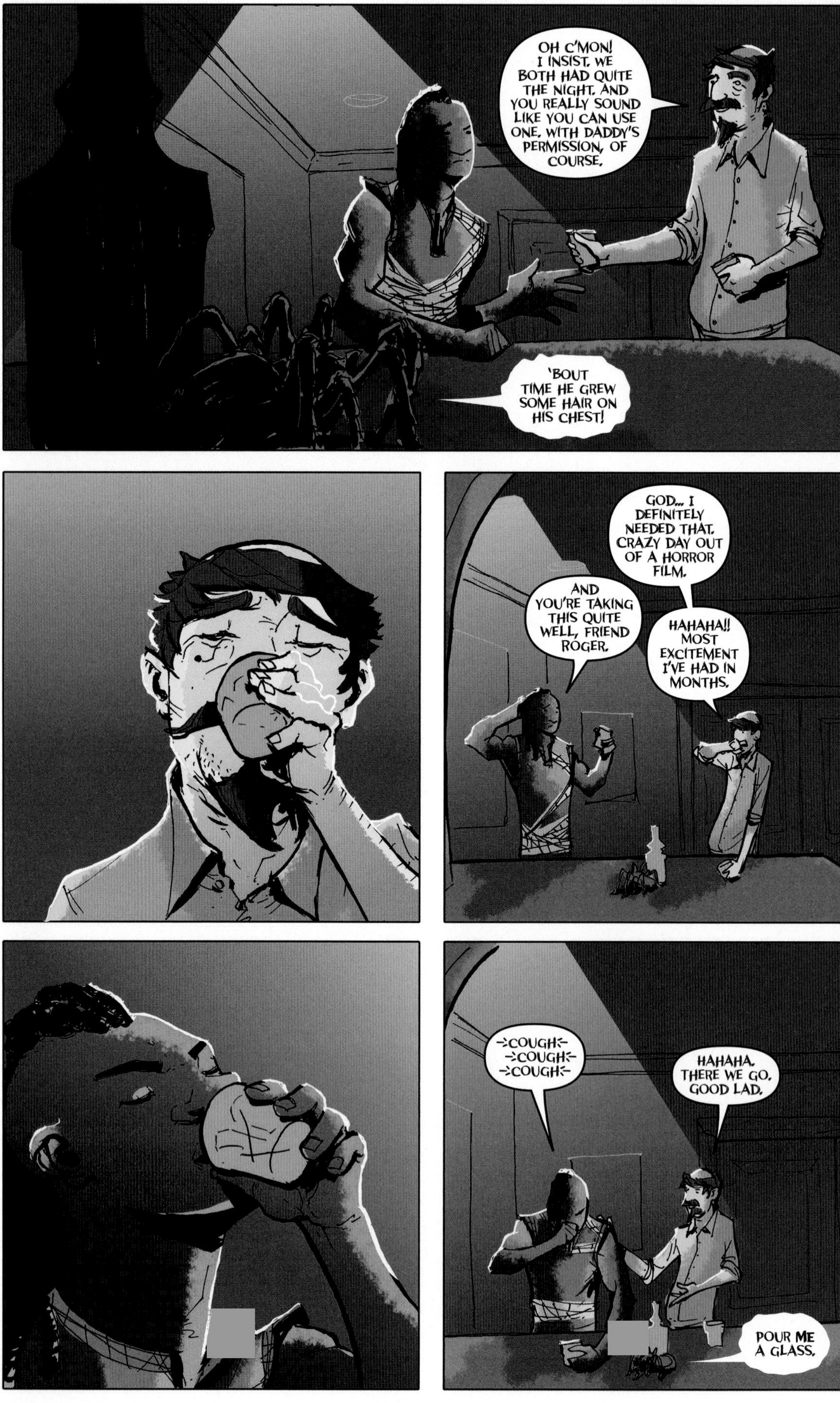
OH C'MON! I INSIST. WE BOTH HAD QUITE THE NIGHT. AND YOU REALLY SOUND LIKE YOU CAN USE ONE. WITH DADDY'S PERMISSION, OF COURSE.
'BOUT TIME HE GREW SOME HAIR ON HIS CHEST!
GOD... I DEFINITELY NEEDED THAT. CRAZY DAY OUT OF A HORROR FILM.
AND YOU'RE TAKING THIS QUITE WELL, FRIEND ROGER.
HAHAHA!! MOST EXCITEMENT I'VE HAD IN MONTHS.
COUGH
COUGH
COUGH
HAHAHA. THERE WE GO, GOOD LAD.
POUR ME A GLASS.

THANK YOU, IS'NANA. I'LL NEVER FORGET WHAT YOU DID FOR ME TONIGHT.

DON'T BEAT YOURSELF UP TOO MUCH. YOU'RE A HERO IN MY EYES... YOU'RE A HERO.

HE ASKED ME NOT TO LEAVE JUST YET AND TO SPEND SOME TIME WITH HIM.

HE TOLD ME STORIES OF HIS PAST AND STORIES THAT EXCITED HIM. HE PLAYED ME STORIES FROM HIS INSTRUMENT CALLED A SAXOPHONE AND ASKED FOR STORIES OF MINE IN RETURN.

YES, THAT IS WONDERFUL, THIS IS WONDERFUL!

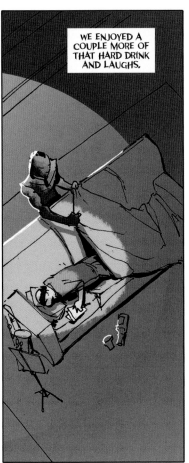

WE ENJOYED A COUPLE MORE OF THAT HARD DRINK AND LAUGHS.

AND HE EVENTUALLY HAD THE TEA THAT MADE HIM GO TO SLEEP. I MADE A FRIEND TONIGHT AND SO DID HE.

AM I TO BE ONE OF THE MANY FORGOTTEN STORIES? OR A LEGEND LIKE MY FATHER.

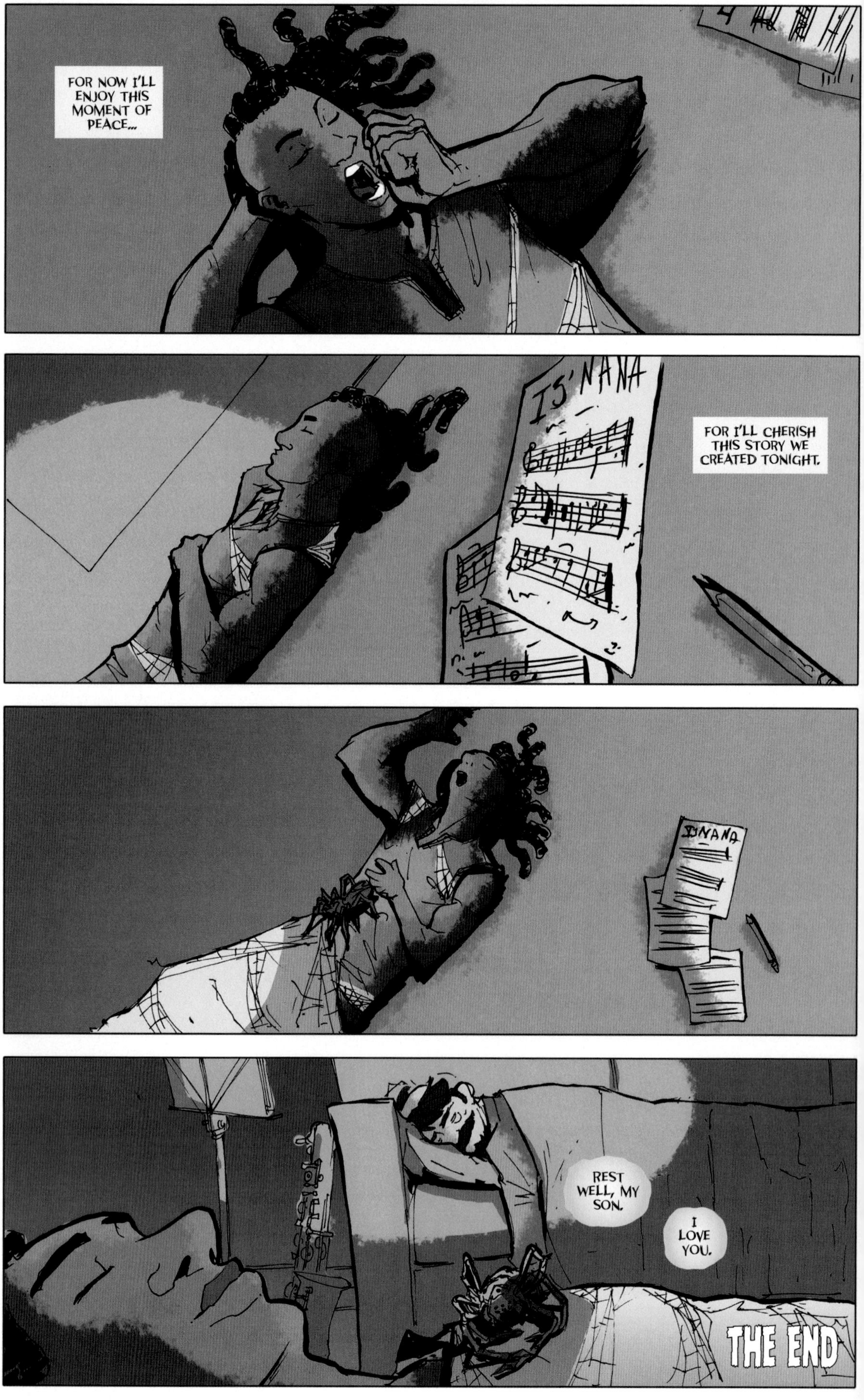
FOR NOW I'LL ENJOY THIS MOMENT OF PEACE...
IS'NANA
FOR I'LL CHERISH THIS STORY WE CREATED TONIGHT.
REST WELL, MY SON.
I LOVE YOU.
THE END

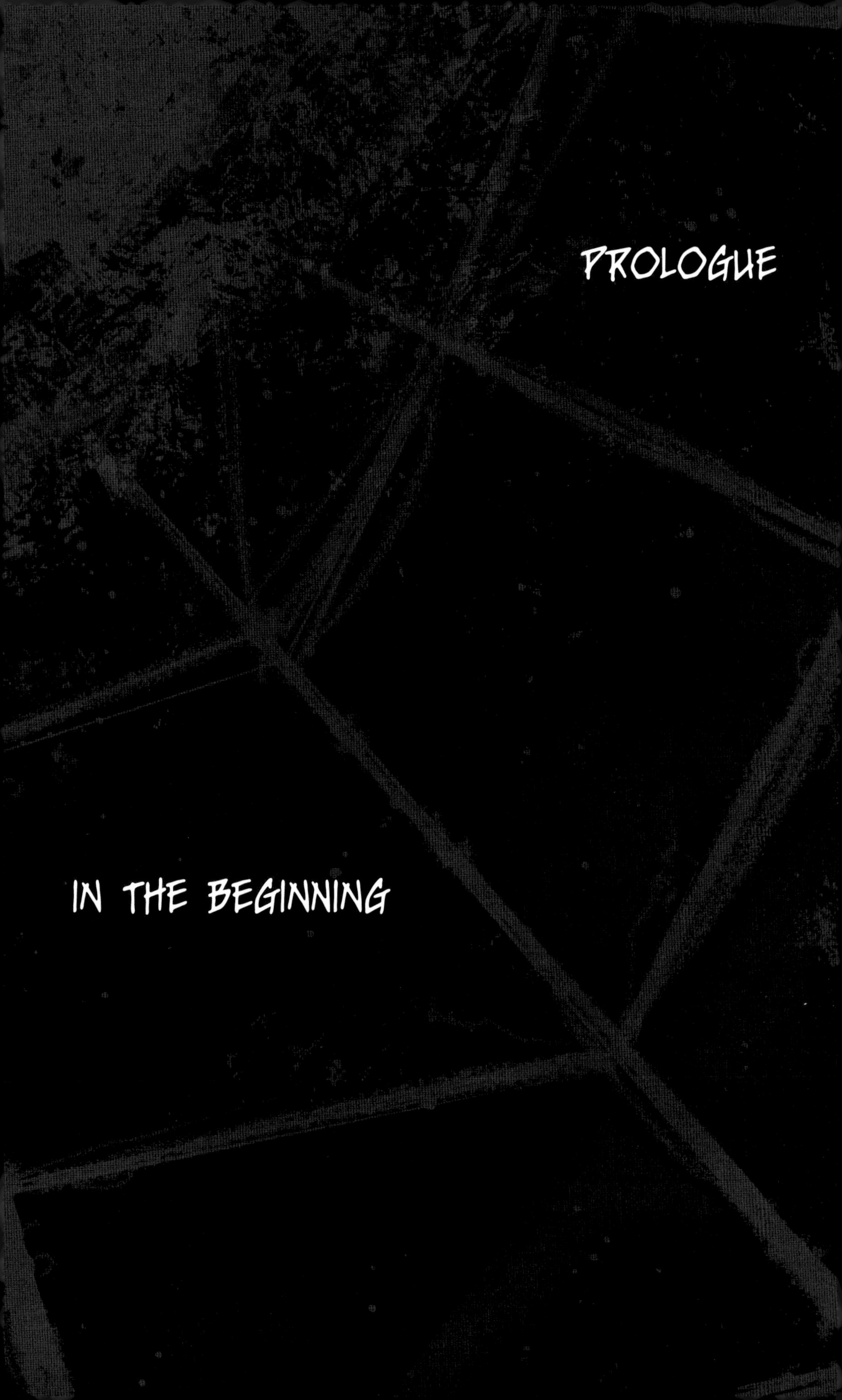
PROLOGUE
IN THE BEGINNING

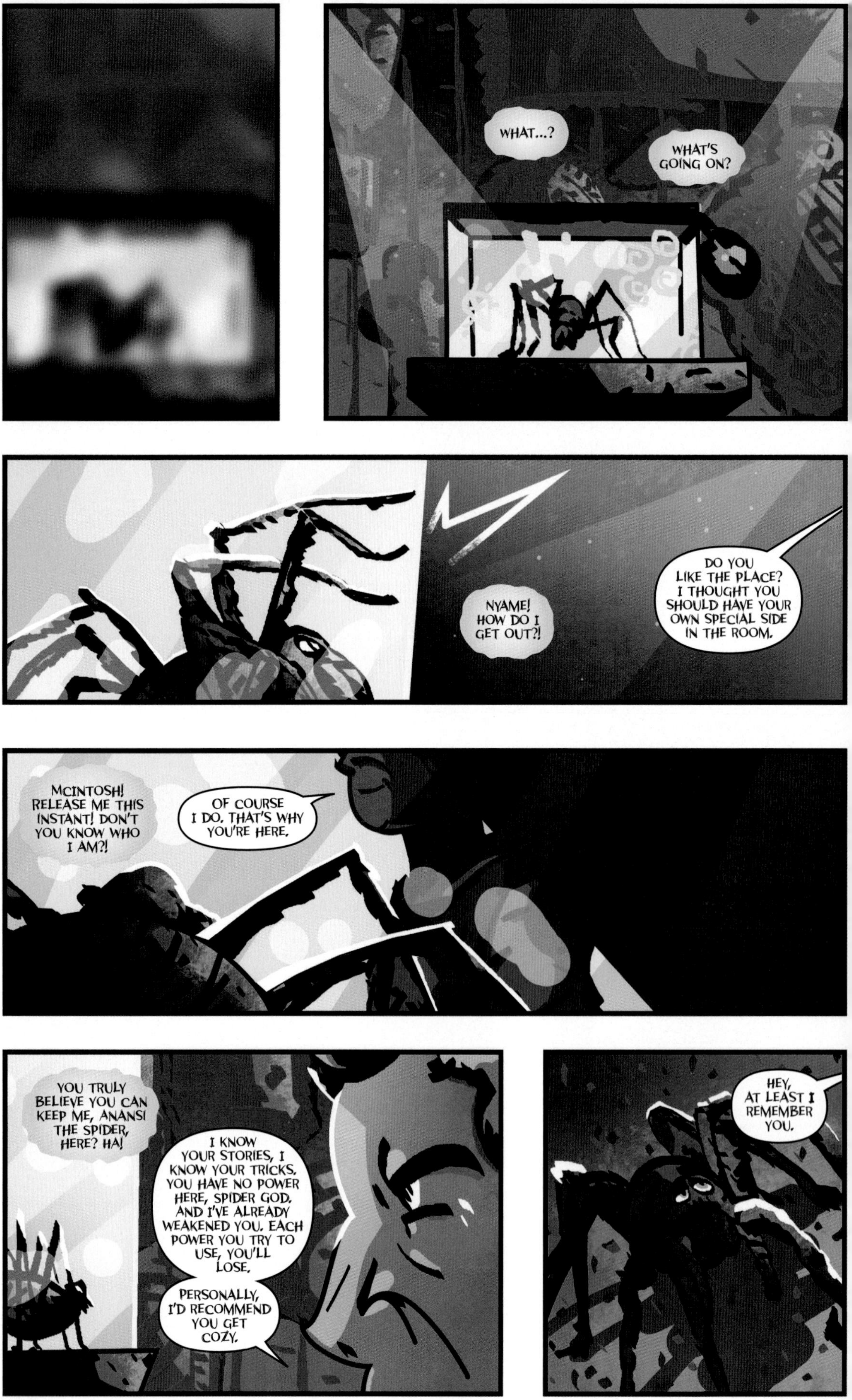

WHAT...?
WHAT'S GOING ON?
NYAME! HOW DO I GET OUT?!
DO YOU LIKE THE PLACE? I THOUGHT YOU SHOULD HAVE YOUR OWN SPECIAL SIDE IN THE ROOM.
MCINTOSH! RELEASE ME THIS INSTANT! DON'T YOU KNOW WHO I AM?!
OF COURSE I DO. THAT'S WHY YOU'RE HERE.
YOU TRULY BELIEVE YOU CAN KEEP ME, ANANSI THE SPIDER, HERE? HA!
I KNOW YOUR STORIES, I KNOW YOUR TRICKS. YOU HAVE NO POWER HERE, SPIDER GOD. AND I'VE ALREADY WEAKENED YOU. EACH POWER YOU TRY TO USE, YOU'LL LOSE.
PERSONALLY, I'D RECOMMEND YOU GET COZY.
HEY, AT LEAST I REMEMBER YOU.

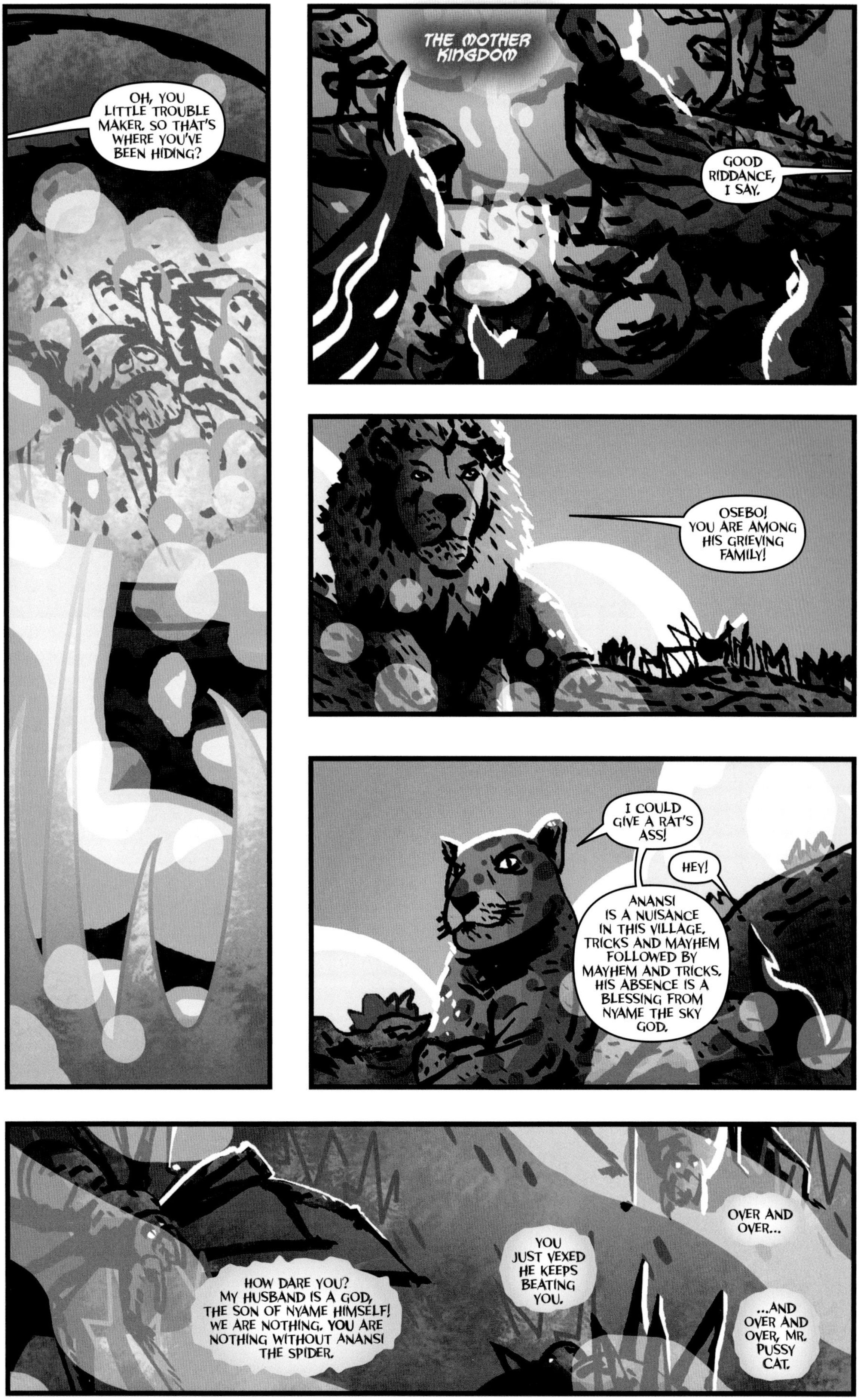
OH, YOU LITTLE TROUBLE MAKER. SO THAT'S WHERE YOU'VE BEEN HIDING?
THE MOTHER KINGDOM
GOOD RIDDANCE, I SAY.
OSEBO! YOU ARE AMONG HIS GRIEVING FAMILY!
I COULD GIVE A RAT'S ASS!
HEY!
ANANSI IS A NUISANCE IN THIS VILLAGE. TRICKS AND MAYHEM FOLLOWED BY MAYHEM AND TRICKS. HIS ABSENCE IS A BLESSING FROM NYAME THE SKY GOD.
HOW DARE YOU? MY HUSBAND IS A GOD, THE SON OF NYAME HIMSELF! WE ARE NOTHING. YOU ARE NOTHING WITHOUT ANANSI THE SPIDER.
YOU JUST VEXED HE KEEPS BEATING YOU.
OVER AND OVER...
...AND OVER AND OVER, MR. PUSSY CAT.

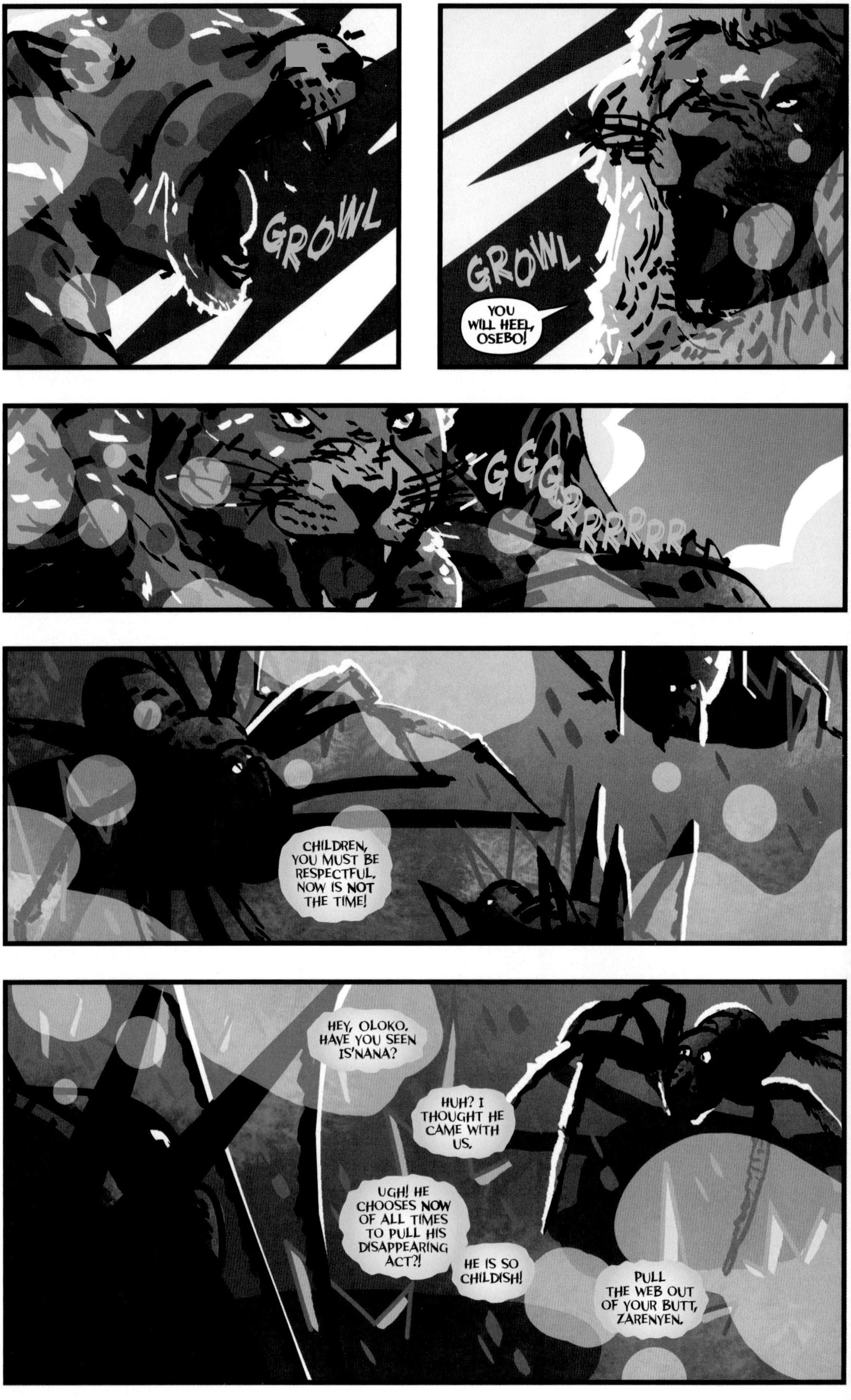
GROWL
GROWL
YOU WILL HEEL, OSEBO!
GGGRRRRRRR
CHILDREN, YOU MUST BE RESPECTFUL. NOW IS NOT THE TIME!
HEY, OLOKO, HAVE YOU SEEN IS'NANA?
HUH? I THOUGHT HE CAME WITH US.
UGH! HE CHOOSES NOW OF ALL TIMES TO PULL HIS DISAPPEARING ACT?!
HE IS SO CHILDISH!
PULL THE WEB OUT OF YOUR BUTT, ZARENYEN.

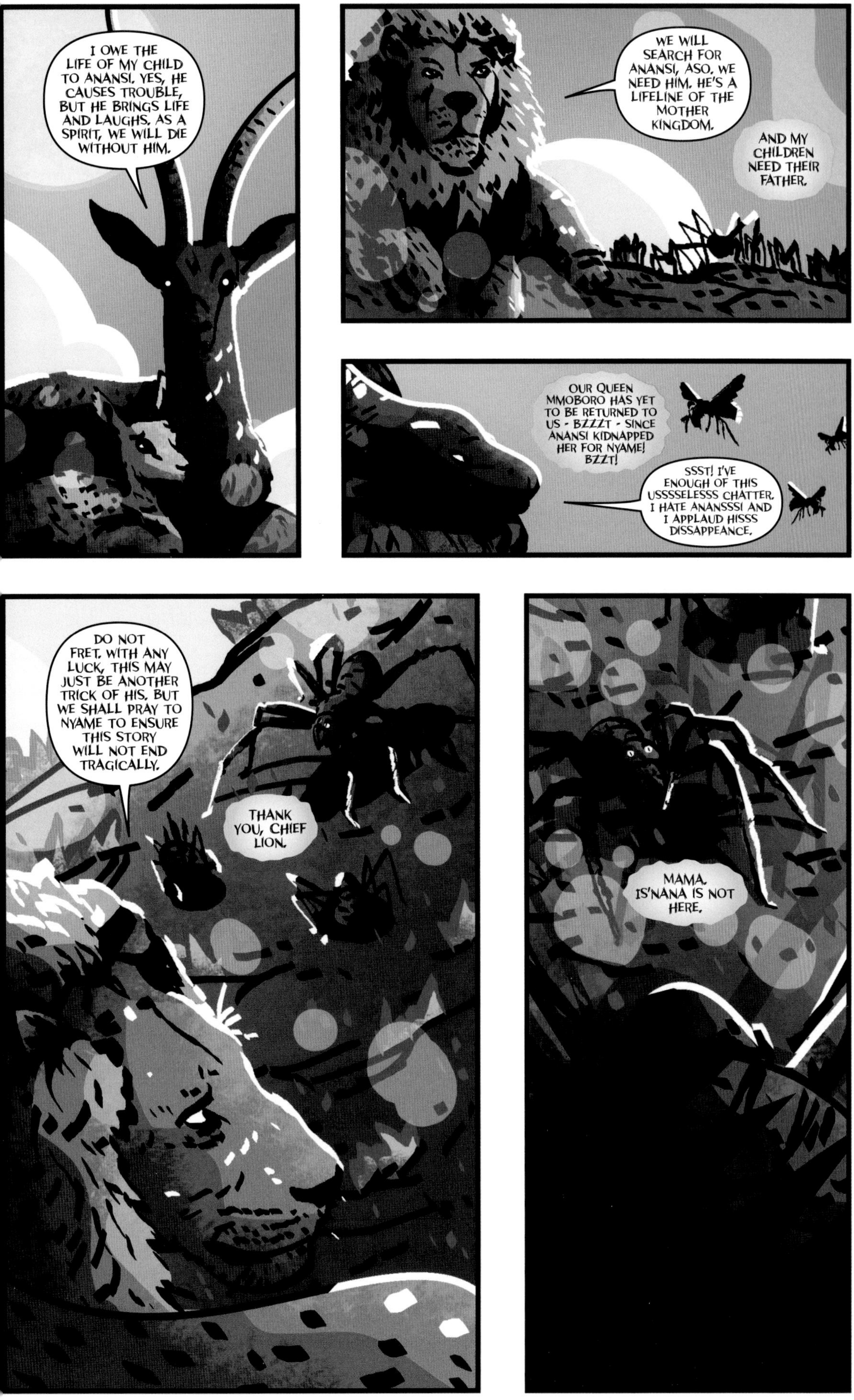
I OWE THE LIFE OF MY CHILD TO ANANSI. YES, HE CAUSES TROUBLE, BUT HE BRINGS LIFE AND LAUGHS. AS A SPIRIT, WE WILL DIE WITHOUT HIM.
WE WILL SEARCH FOR ANANSI, ASO. WE NEED HIM. HE'S A LIFELINE OF THE MOTHER KINGDOM.
AND MY CHILDREN NEED THEIR FATHER.
OUR QUEEN MMOBORO HAS YET TO BE RETURNED TO US - BZZZT - SINCE ANANSI KIDNAPPED HER FOR NYAME! BZZT!
SSST! I'VE ENOUGH OF THIS USSSSELESSS CHATTER. I HATE ANANSSSI AND I APPLAUD HISSS DISSAPPEANCE.
DO NOT FRET. WITH ANY LUCK, THIS MAY JUST BE ANOTHER TRICK OF HIS. BUT WE SHALL PRAY TO NYAME TO ENSURE THIS STORY WILL NOT END TRAGICALLY.
THANK YOU, CHIEF LION.
MAMA. IS'NANA IS NOT HERE.

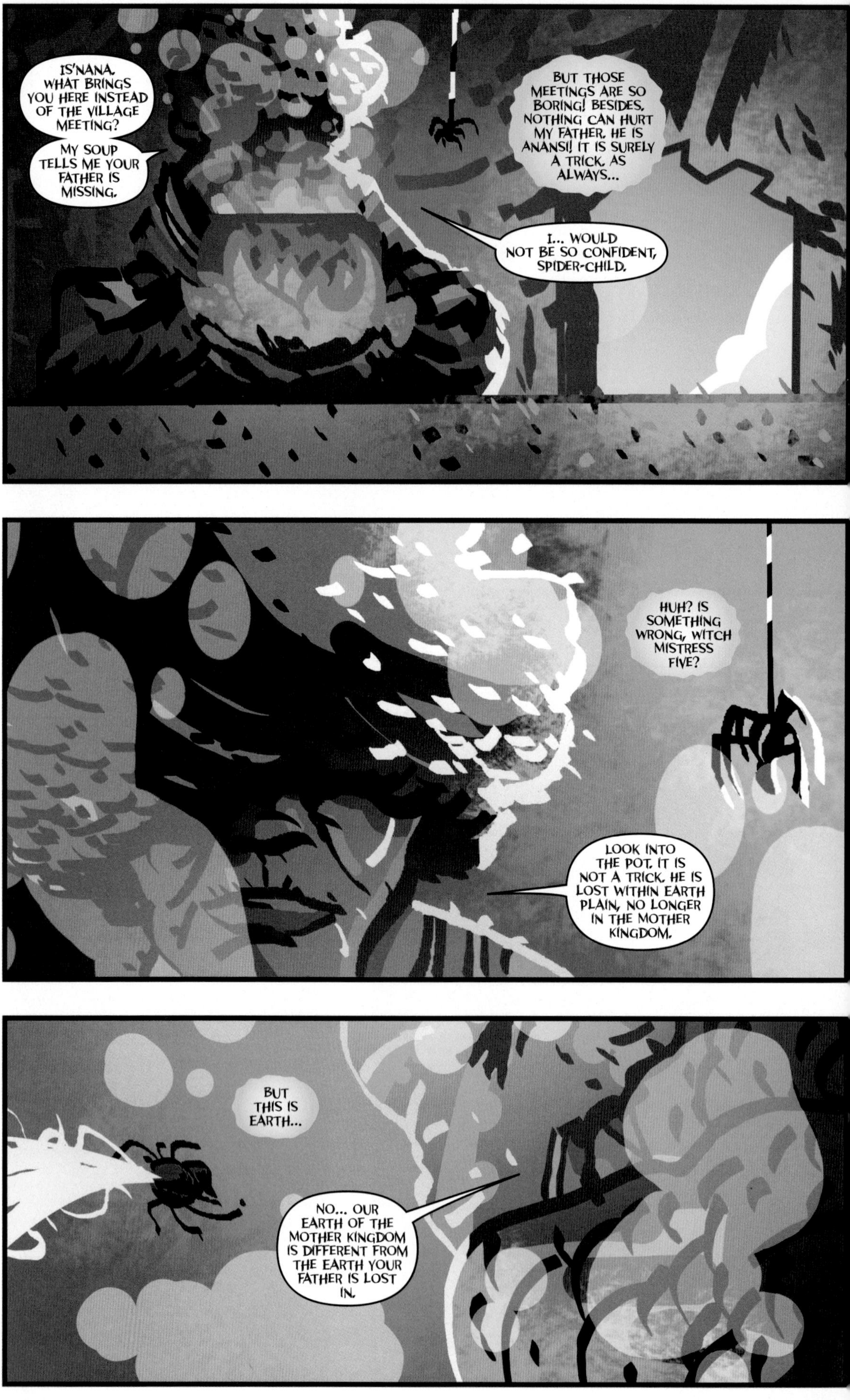
IS'NANA. WHAT BRINGS YOU HERE INSTEAD OF THE VILLAGE MEETING?
MY SOUP TELLS ME YOUR FATHER IS MISSING.
BUT THOSE MEETINGS ARE SO BORING! BESIDES. NOTHING CAN HURT MY FATHER. HE IS ANANSI! IT IS SURELY A TRICK. AS ALWAYS...
I... WOULD NOT BE SO CONFIDENT, SPIDER-CHILD.
HUH? IS SOMETHING WRONG, WITCH MISTRESS FIVE?
LOOK INTO THE POT. IT IS NOT A TRICK. HE IS LOST WITHIN EARTH PLAIN, NO LONGER IN THE MOTHER KINGDOM.
BUT THIS IS EARTH...
NO... OUR EARTH OF THE MOTHER KINGDOM IS DIFFERENT FROM THE EARTH YOUR FATHER IS LOST IN.

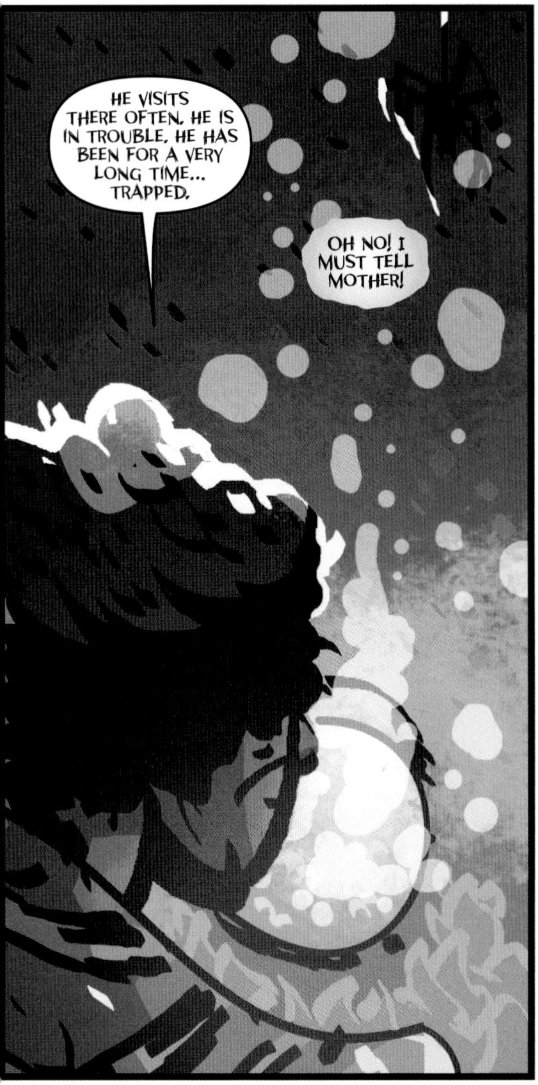
HE VISITS THERE OFTEN. HE IS IN TROUBLE. HE HAS BEEN FOR A VERY LONG TIME... TRAPPED.
OH NO! I MUST TELL MOTHER!

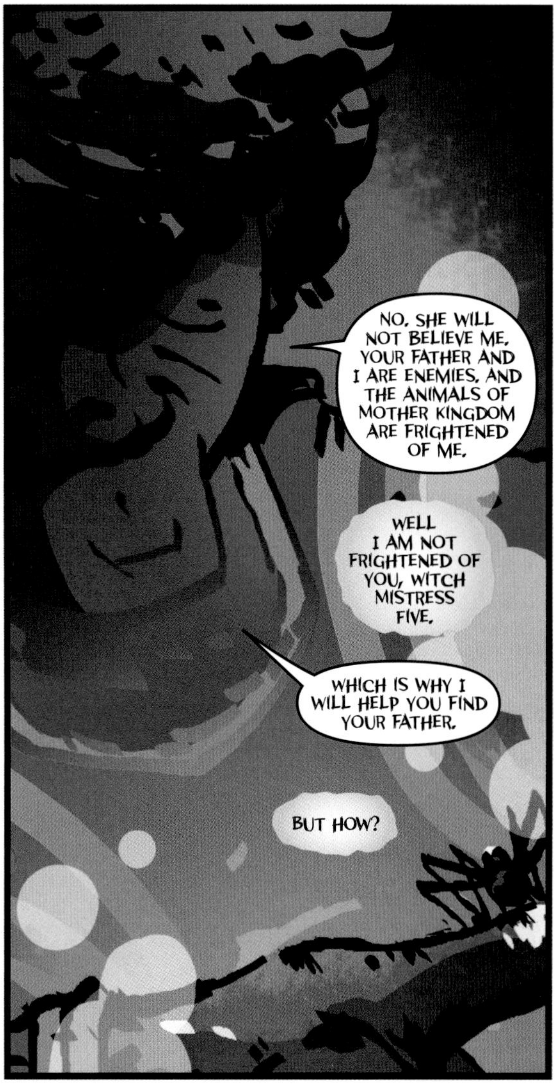
NO. SHE WILL NOT BELIEVE ME. YOUR FATHER AND I ARE ENEMIES. AND THE ANIMALS OF MOTHER KINGDOM ARE FRIGHTENED OF ME.
WELL I AM NOT FRIGHTENED OF YOU, WITCH MISTRESS FIVE.
WHICH IS WHY I WILL HELP YOU FIND YOUR FATHER.
BUT HOW?

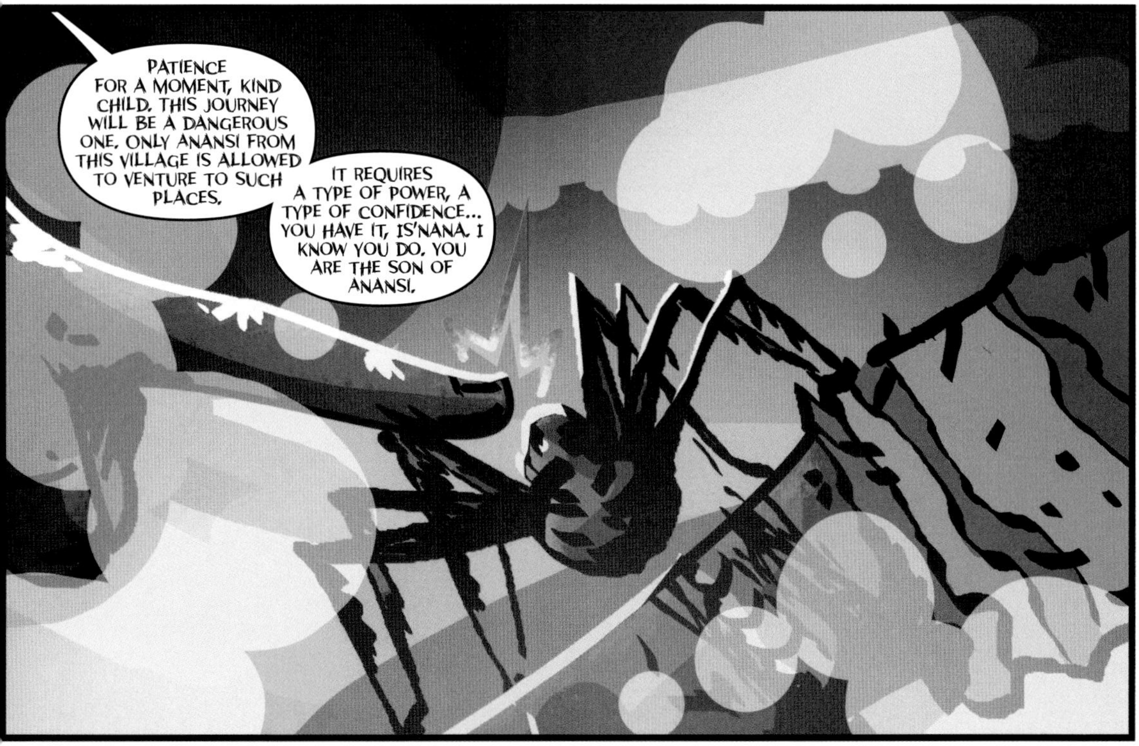
PATIENCE FOR A MOMENT, KIND CHILD. THIS JOURNEY WILL BE A DANGEROUS ONE. ONLY ANANSI FROM THIS VILLAGE IS ALLOWED TO VENTURE TO SUCH PLACES.
IT REQUIRES A TYPE OF POWER, A TYPE OF CONFIDENCE... YOU HAVE IT, IS'NANA. I KNOW YOU DO. YOU ARE THE SON OF ANANSI.

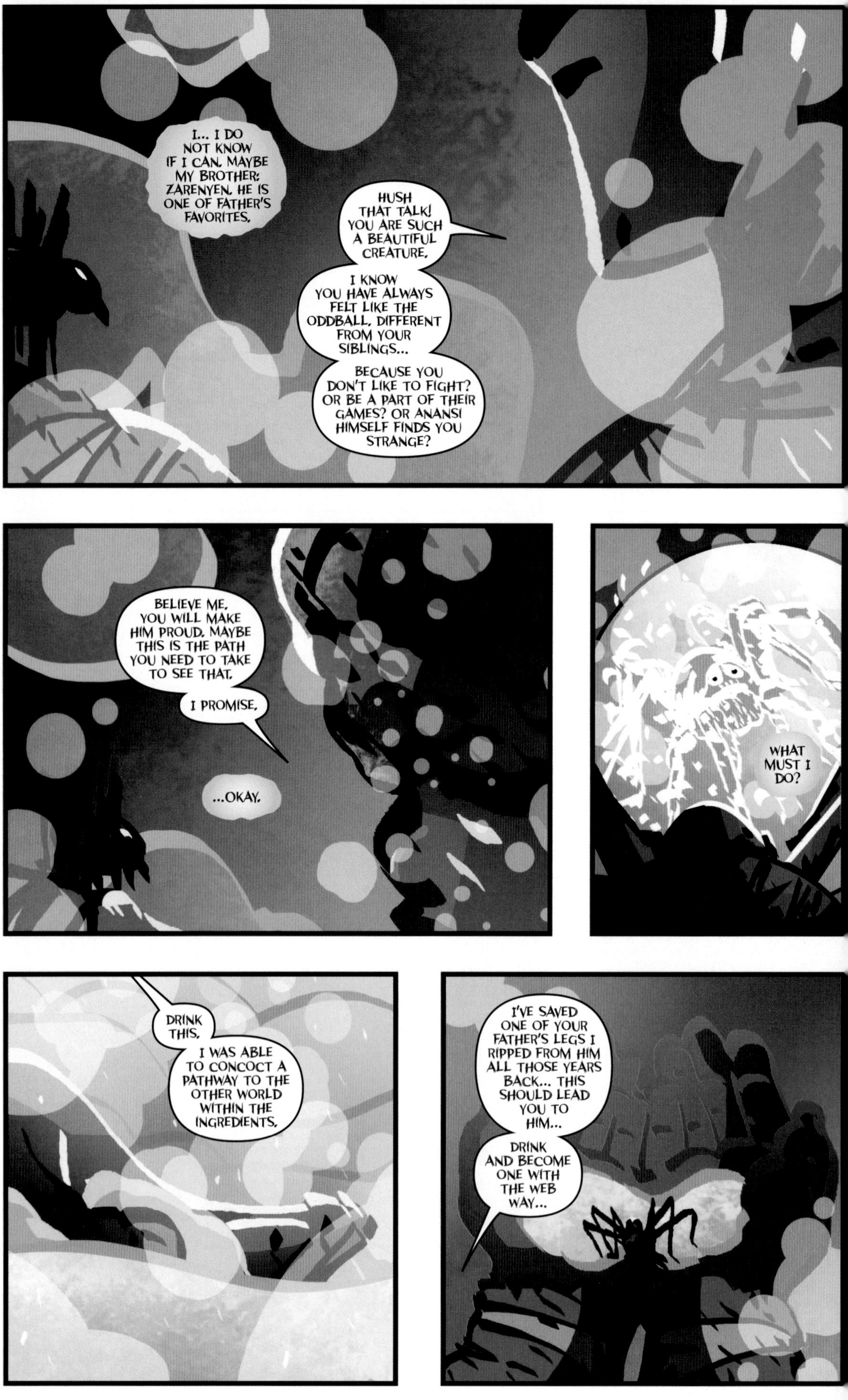
I... I DO NOT KNOW IF I CAN. MAYBE MY BROTHER: ZARENYEN. HE IS ONE OF FATHER'S FAVORITES.
HUSH THAT TALK! YOU ARE SUCH A BEAUTIFUL CREATURE.
I KNOW YOU HAVE ALWAYS FELT LIKE THE ODDBALL. DIFFERENT FROM YOUR SIBLINGS...
BECAUSE YOU DON'T LIKE TO FIGHT? OR BE A PART OF THEIR GAMES? OR ANANSI HIMSELF FINDS YOU STRANGE?
BELIEVE ME, YOU WILL MAKE HIM PROUD. MAYBE THIS IS THE PATH YOU NEED TO TAKE TO SEE THAT.
I PROMISE.
...OKAY.
WHAT MUST I DO?
DRINK THIS.
I WAS ABLE TO CONCOCT A PATHWAY TO THE OTHER WORLD WITHIN THE INGREDIENTS.
I'VE SAVED ONE OF YOUR FATHER'S LEGS I RIPPED FROM HIM ALL THOSE YEARS BACK... THIS SHOULD LEAD YOU TO HIM...
DRINK AND BECOME ONE WITH THE WEB WAY...

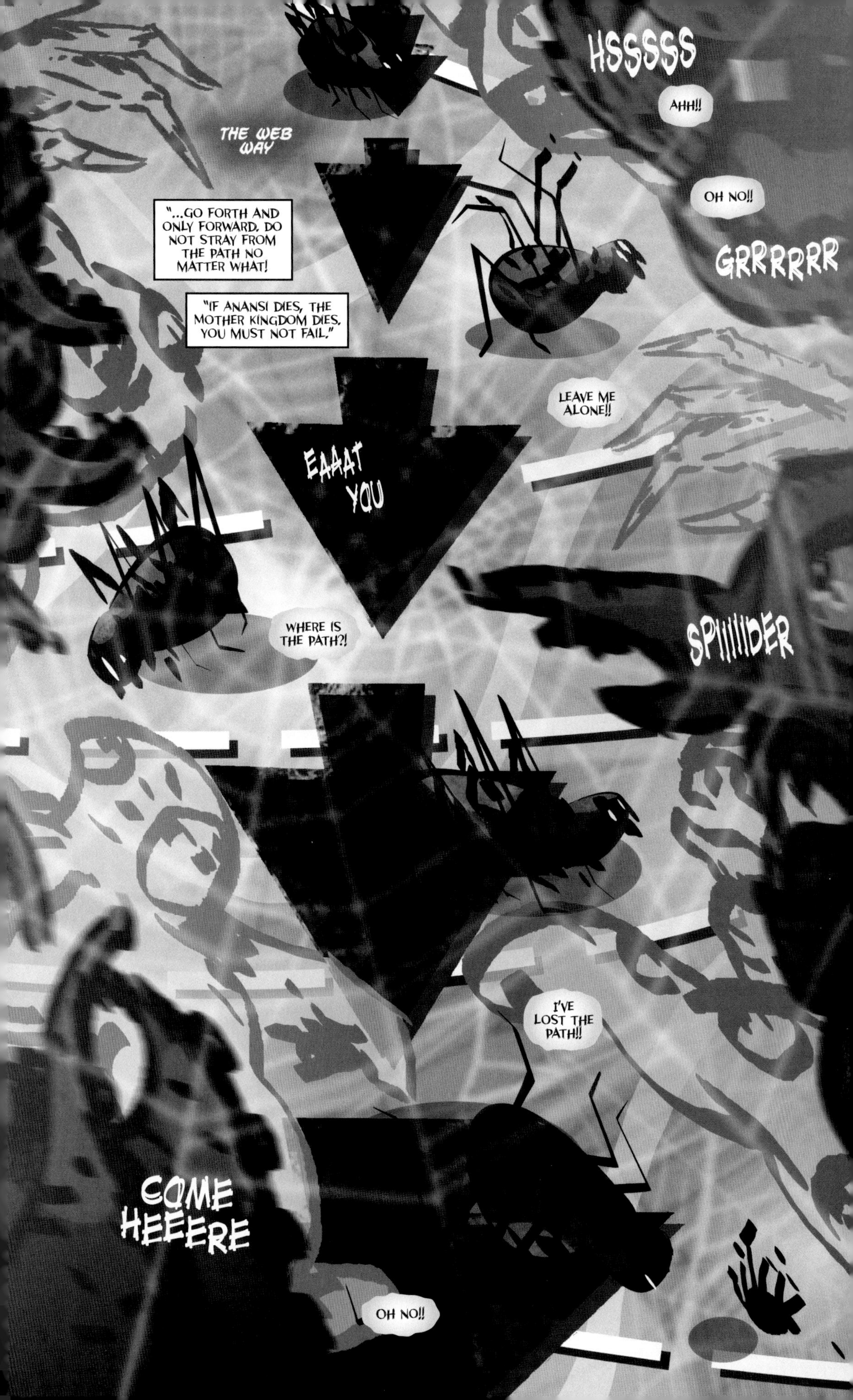

THE WEB WAY
"...GO FORTH AND ONLY FORWARD. DO NOT STRAY FROM THE PATH NO MATTER WHAT!
"IF ANANSI DIES, THE MOTHER KINGDOM DIES. YOU MUST NOT FAIL."
HSSSSS
AHH!!
OH NO!!
GRRRRRR
LEAVE ME ALONE!!
EAAAT YOU
WHERE IS THE PATH?!
SPIIIIIDER
I'VE LOST THE PATH!!
COME HEEERE
OH NO!!

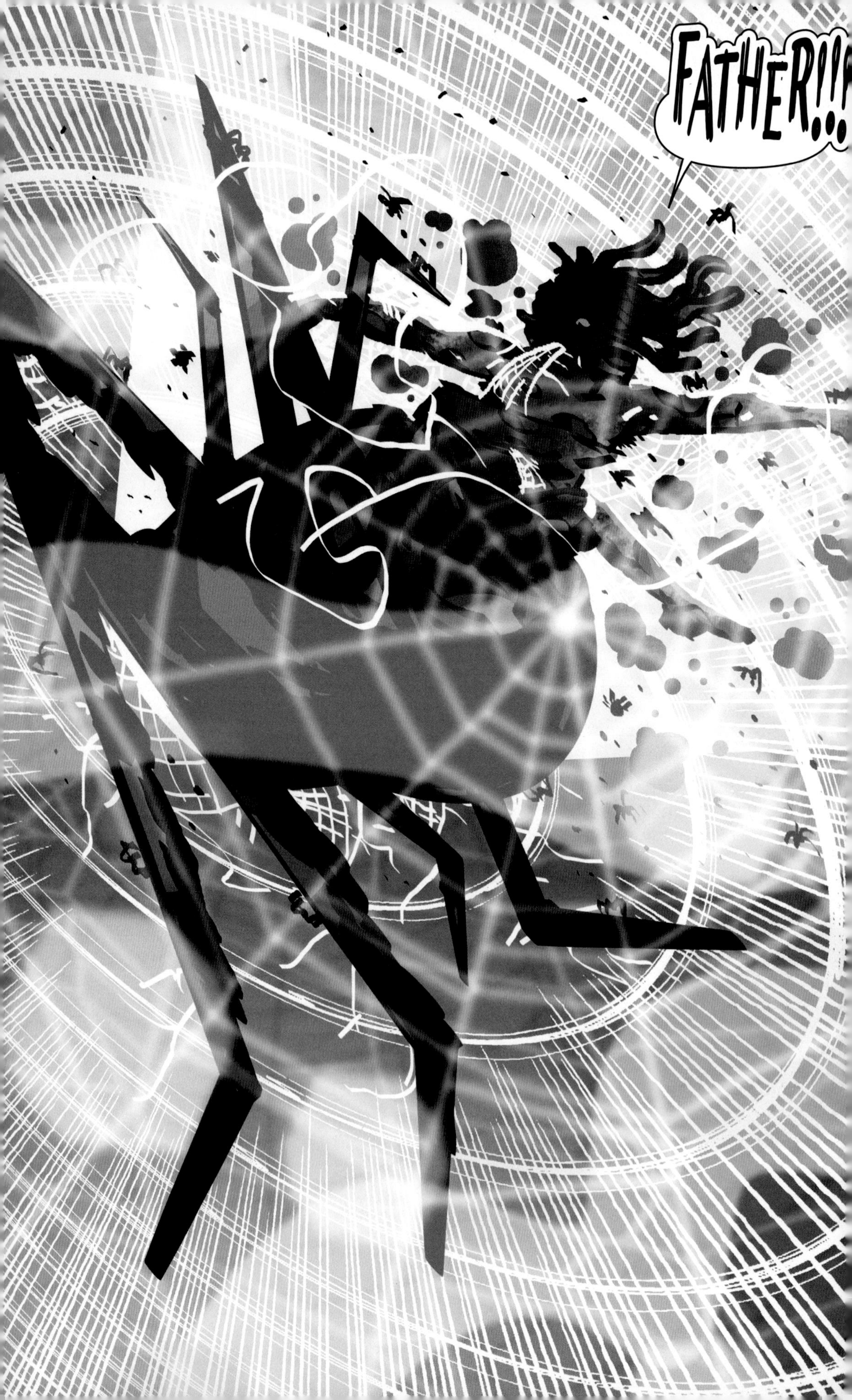
FATHER!!!

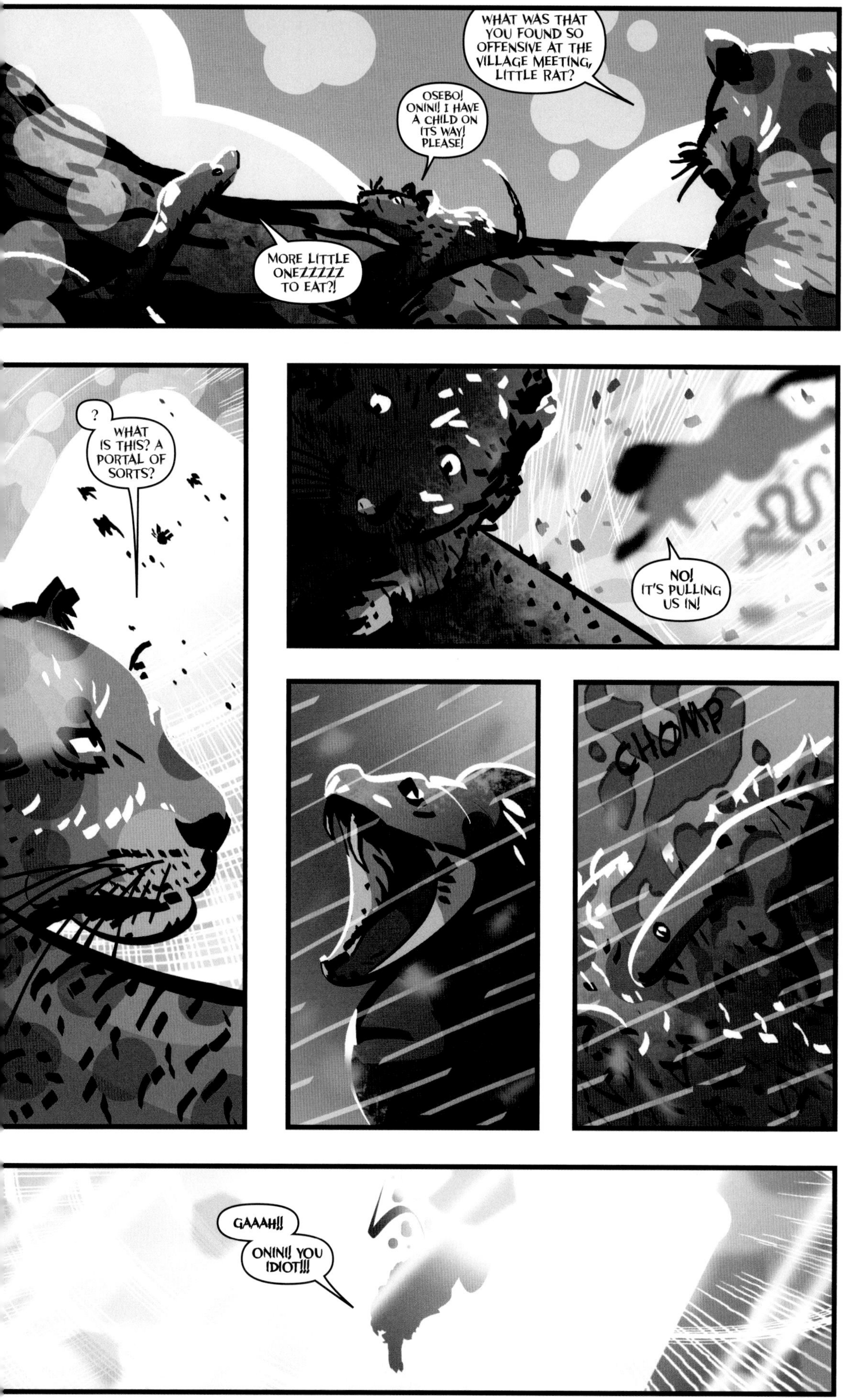
WHAT WAS THAT YOU FOUND SO OFFENSIVE AT THE VILLAGE MEETING, LITTLE RAT?
OSEBO! ONINI! I HAVE A CHILD ON ITS WAY! PLEASE!
MORE LITTLE ONEZZZZZ TO EAT?!
?
WHAT IS THIS? A PORTAL OF SORTS?
NO! IT'S PULLING US IN!
CHOMP
GAAAH!!
ONINI! YOU IDIOT!!!

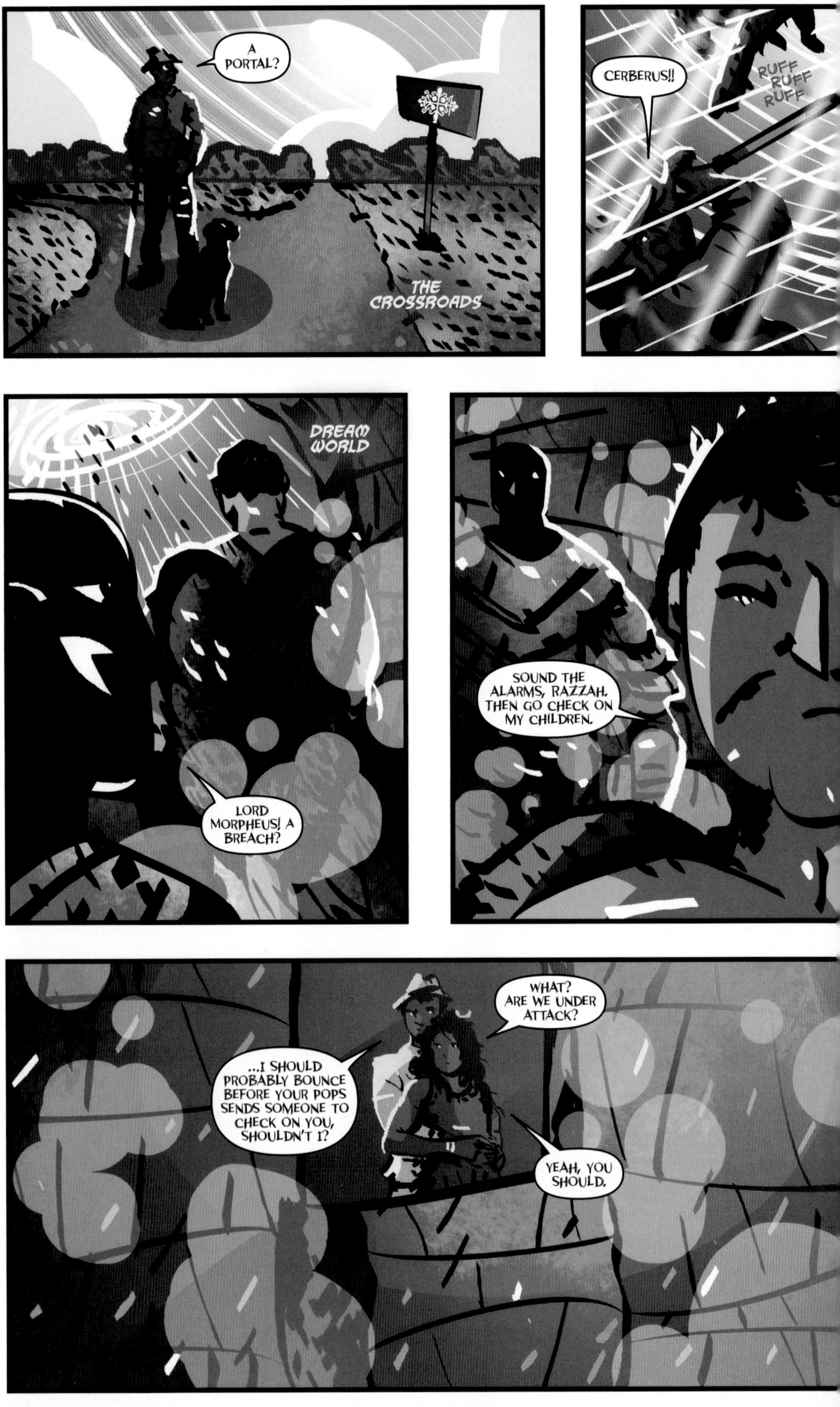
A PORTAL?
THE CROSSROADS
CERBERUS!!
RUFF RUFF RUFF
DREAM WORLD
LORD MORPHEUS! A BREACH?
SOUND THE ALARMS, RAZZAH. THEN GO CHECK ON MY CHILDREN.
WHAT? ARE WE UNDER ATTACK?
...I SHOULD PROBABLY BOUNCE BEFORE YOUR POPS SENDS SOMEONE TO CHECK ON YOU, SHOULDN'T I?
YEAH, YOU SHOULD.

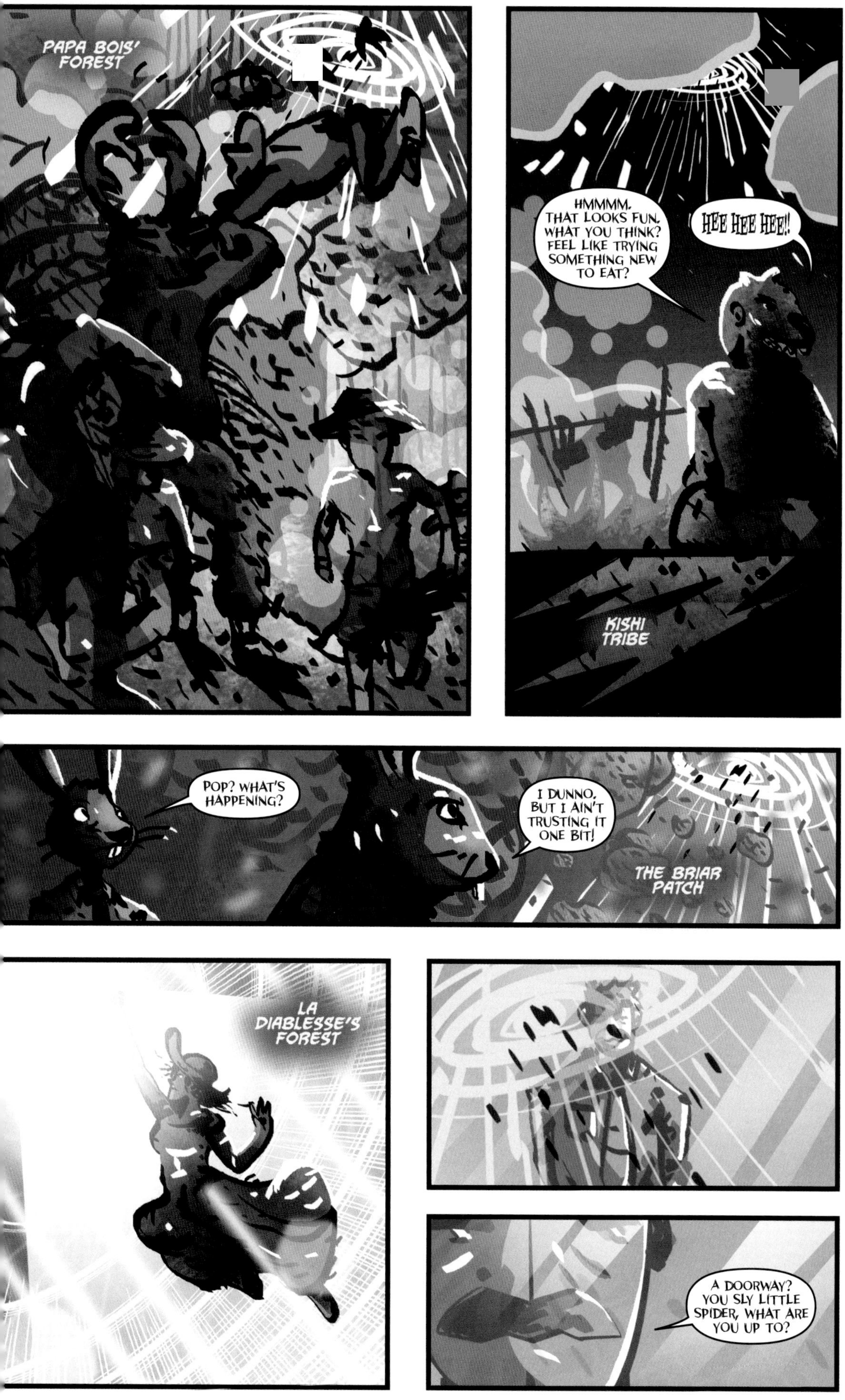
PAPA BOIS' FOREST
HMMMM. THAT LOOKS FUN. WHAT YOU THINK? FEEL LIKE TRYING SOMETHING NEW TO EAT?
HEE HEE HEE!!
KISHI TRIBE
POP? WHAT'S HAPPENING?
I DUNNO, BUT I AIN'T TRUSTING IT ONE BIT!
THE BRIAR PATCH
LA DIABLESSE'S FOREST
A DOORWAY? YOU SLY LITTLE SPIDER, WHAT ARE YOU UP TO?

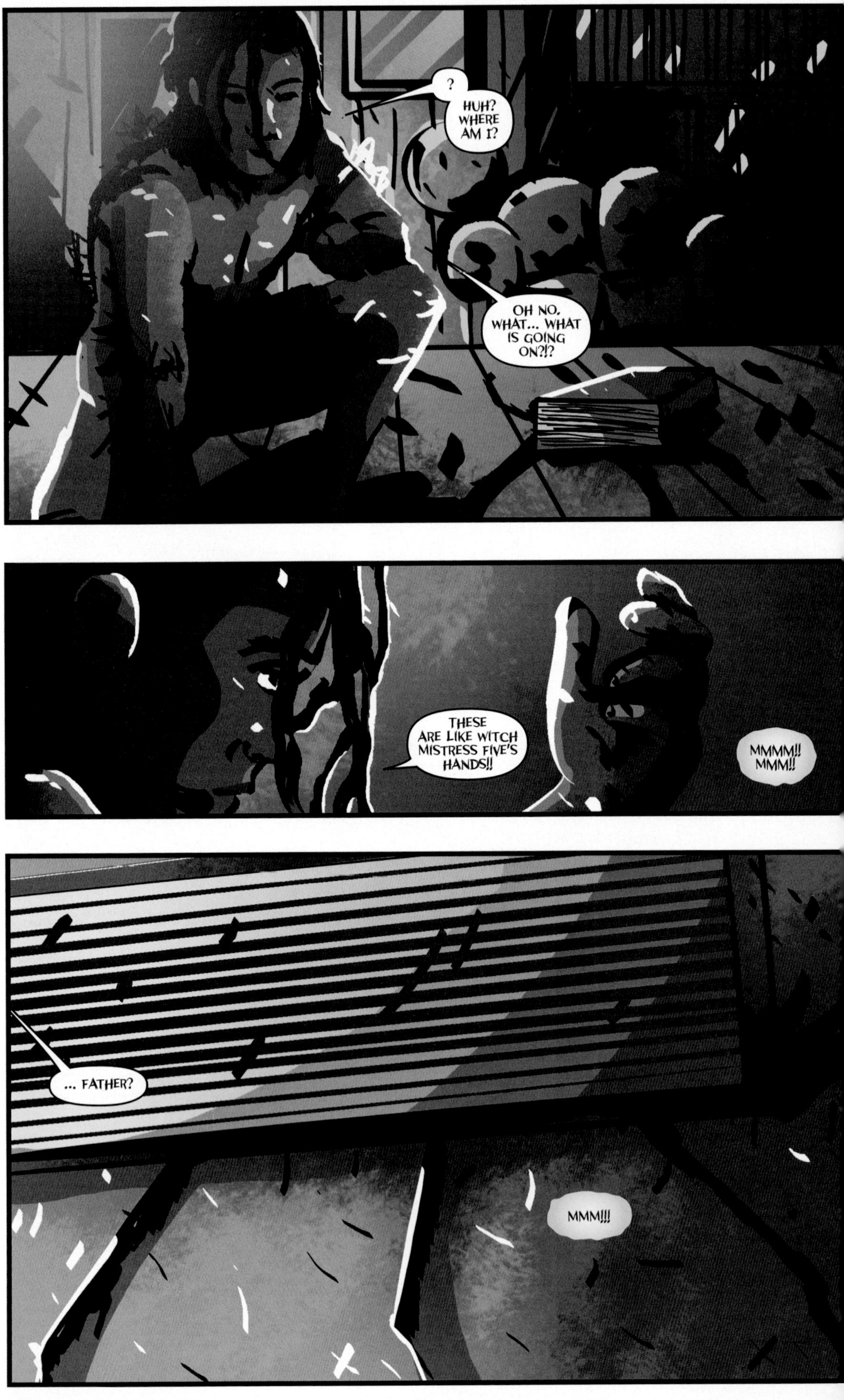
?
HUH? WHERE AM I?
OH NO. WHAT... WHAT IS GOING ON?!?
THESE ARE LIKE WITCH MISTRESS FIVE'S HANDS!!
MMMM!! MMM!!
... FATHER?
MMM!!!

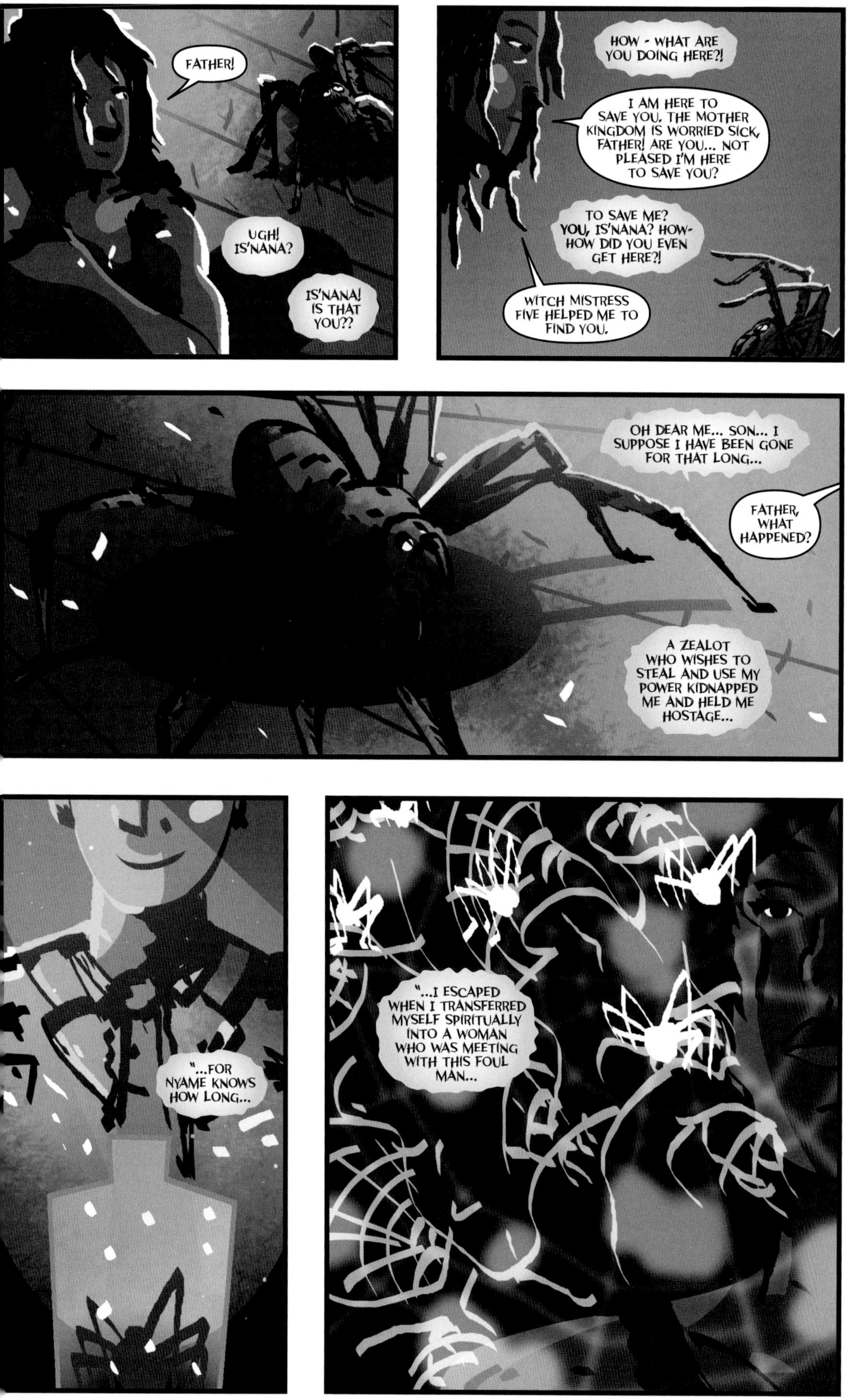
FATHER!
UGH! IS'NANA?
IS'NANA! IS THAT YOU??
HOW - WHAT ARE YOU DOING HERE?!
I AM HERE TO SAVE YOU. THE MOTHER KINGDOM IS WORRIED SICK, FATHER! ARE YOU... NOT PLEASED I'M HERE TO SAVE YOU?
TO SAVE ME? YOU, IS'NANA? HOW-HOW DID YOU EVEN GET HERE?!
WITCH MISTRESS FIVE HELPED ME TO FIND YOU.
OH DEAR ME... SON... I SUPPOSE I HAVE BEEN GONE FOR THAT LONG...
FATHER, WHAT HAPPENED?
A ZEALOT WHO WISHES TO STEAL AND USE MY POWER KIDNAPPED ME AND HELD ME HOSTAGE...
"...FOR NYAME KNOWS HOW LONG...
"...I ESCAPED WHEN I TRANSFERRED MYSELF SPIRITUALLY INTO A WOMAN WHO WAS MEETING WITH THIS FOUL MAN...

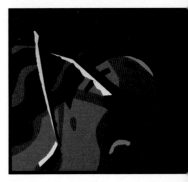

"...THE WOMAN THAT OWNS THIS APARTMENT.

"AFTER TAKING SOME TIME TO RECUPERATE, I WAS TRYING TO COME BACK HOME...

"...IT TOOK SO MUCH OUT OF ME TRYING TO FIND AN ANCHOR.

"IT NEARLY KILLED ME.

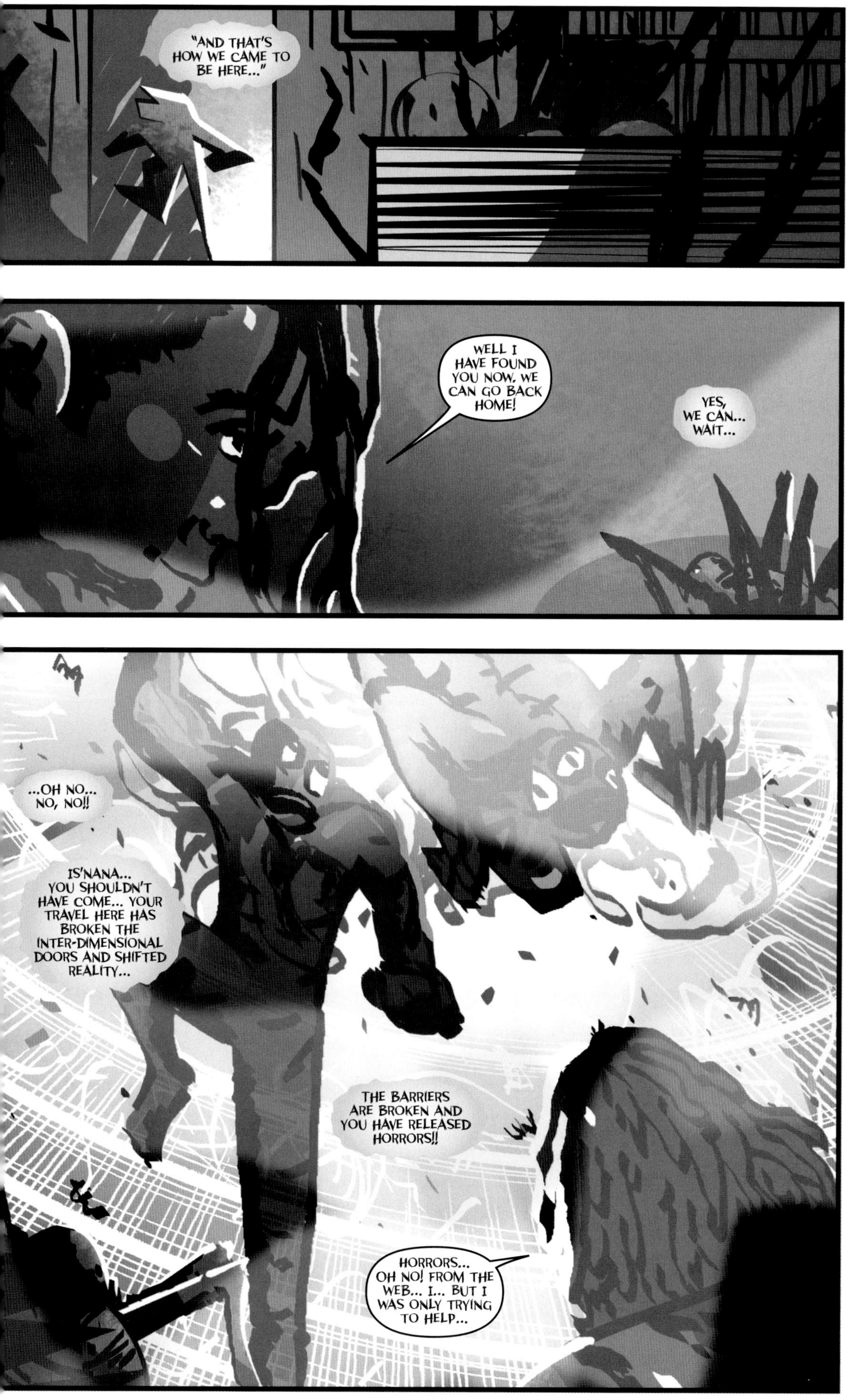
"AND THAT'S HOW WE CAME TO BE HERE..."
WELL I HAVE FOUND YOU NOW. WE CAN GO BACK HOME!
YES, WE CAN... WAIT...
...OH NO... NO, NO!!
IS'NANA... YOU SHOULDN'T HAVE COME... YOUR TRAVEL HERE HAS BROKEN THE INTER-DIMENSIONAL DOORS AND SHIFTED REALITY...
THE BARRIERS ARE BROKEN AND YOU HAVE RELEASED HORRORS!!
HORRORS... OH NO! FROM THE WEB... I... BUT I WAS ONLY TRYING TO HELP...

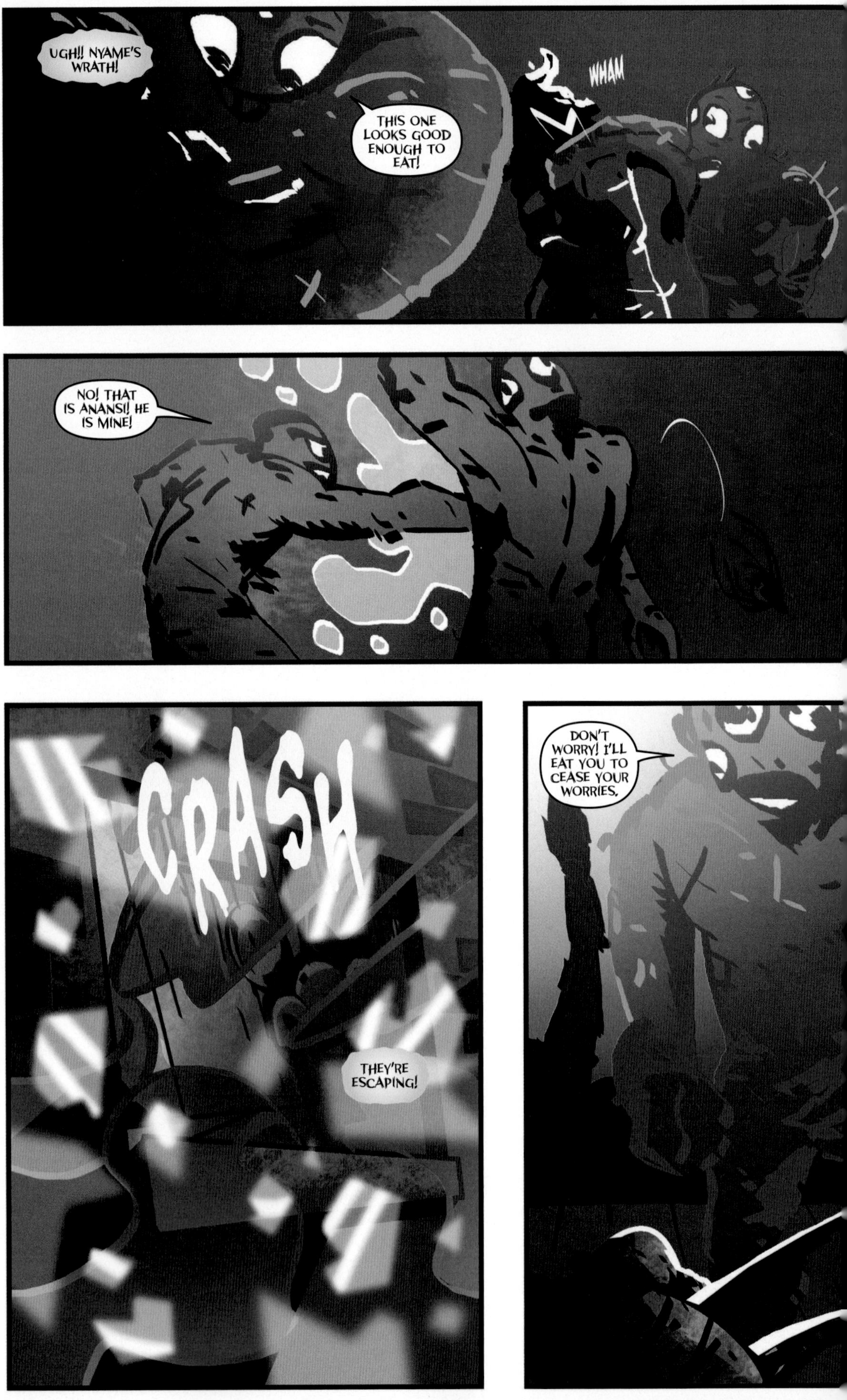
UGH!! NYAME'S WRATH!
THIS ONE LOOKS GOOD ENOUGH TO EAT!
WHAM
NO! THAT IS ANANSI! HE IS MINE!
CRASH
THEY'RE ESCAPING!
DON'T WORRY! I'LL EAT YOU TO CEASE YOUR WORRIES.

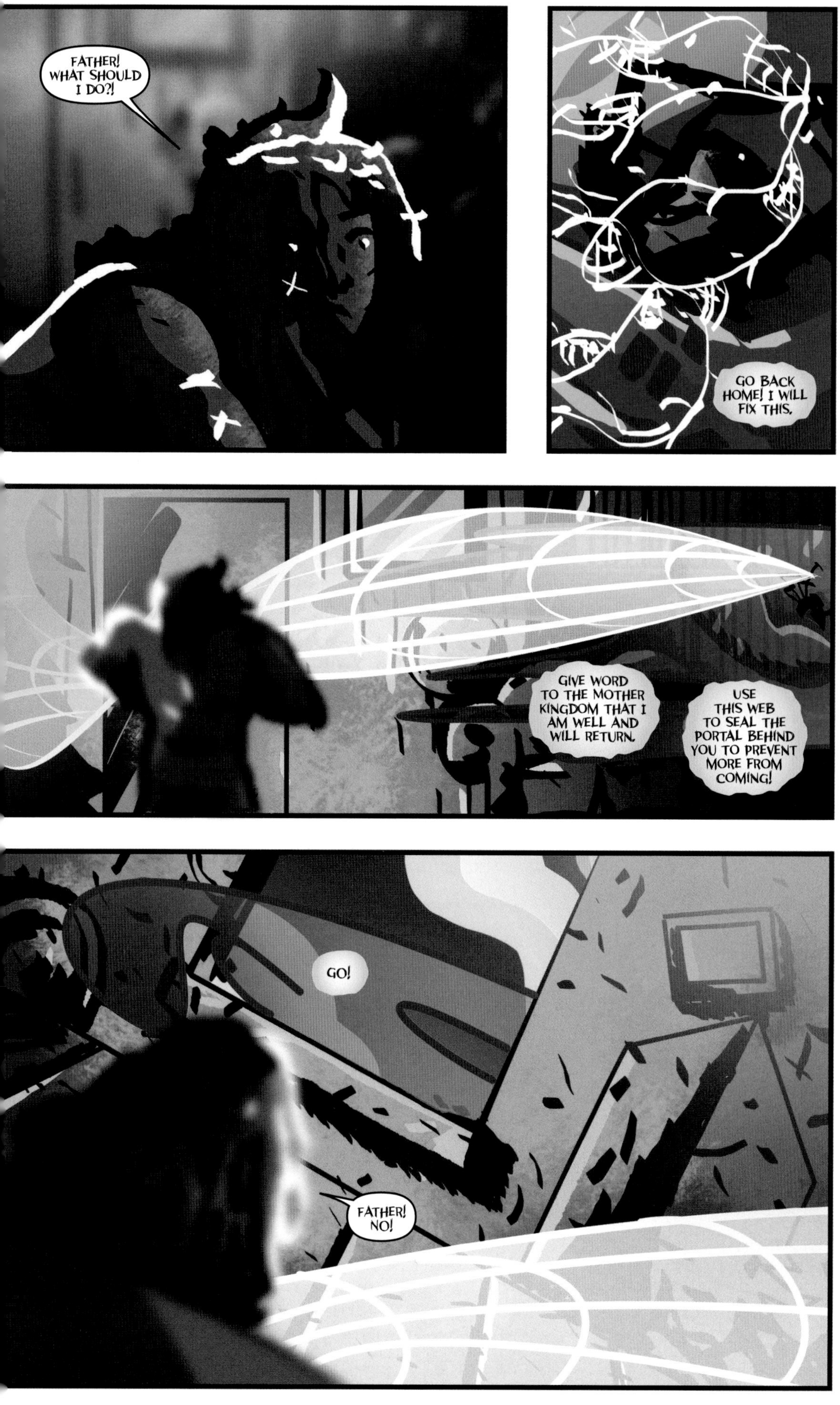
FATHER! WHAT SHOULD I DO?!
GO BACK HOME! I WILL FIX THIS.
GIVE WORD TO THE MOTHER KINGDOM THAT I AM WELL AND WILL RETURN.
USE THIS WEB TO SEAL THE PORTAL BEHIND YOU TO PREVENT MORE FROM COMING!
GO!
FATHER! NO!

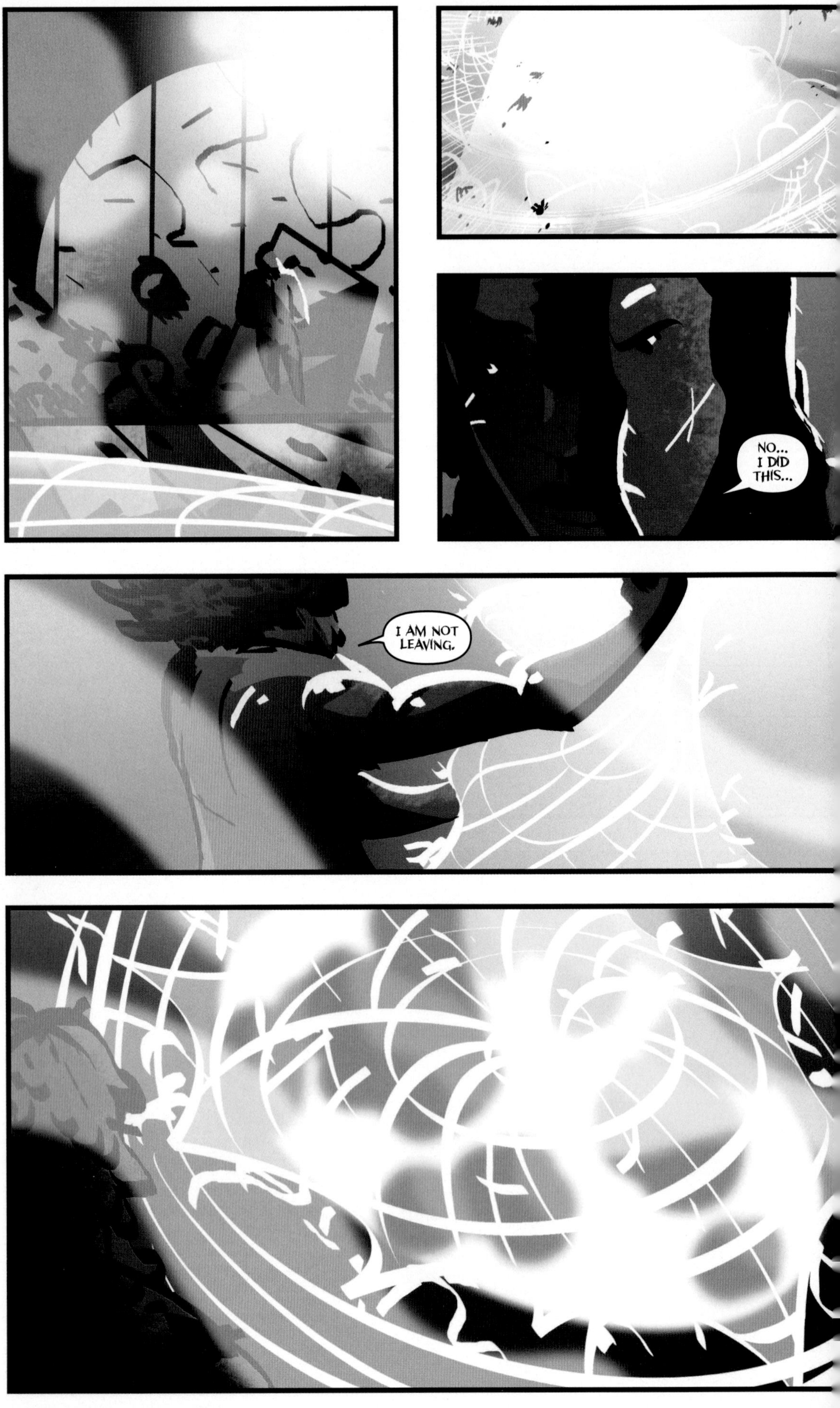
NO...
I DID
THIS...
I AM NOT
LEAVING.

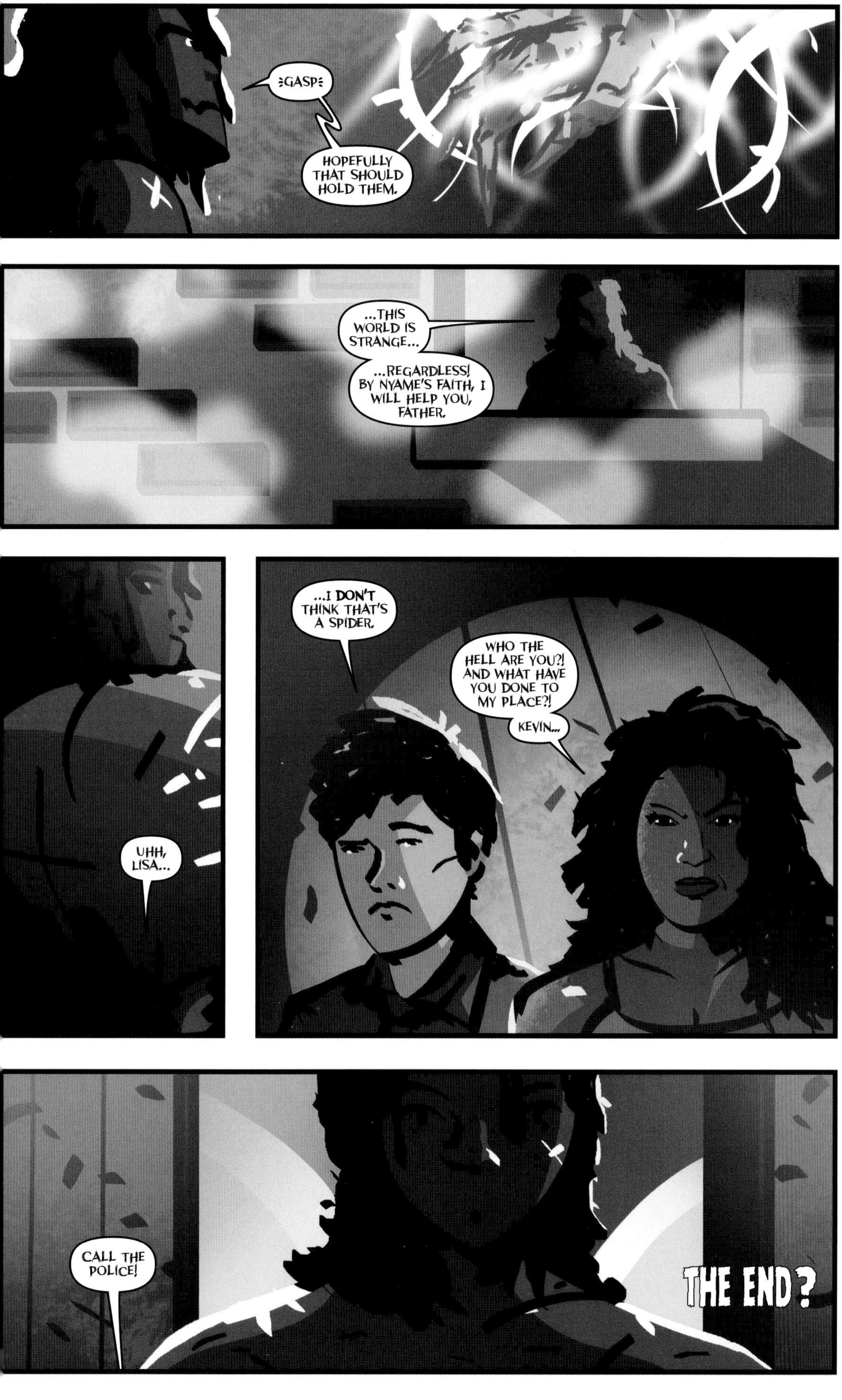
GASP
HOPEFULLY THAT SHOULD HOLD THEM.
...THIS WORLD IS STRANGE...
...REGARDLESS! BY NYAME'S FAITH, I WILL HELP YOU, FATHER.
UHH, LISA...
...I DON'T THINK THAT'S A SPIDER.
WHO THE HELL ARE YOU?! AND WHAT HAVE YOU DONE TO MY PLACE?!
KEVIN...
CALL THE POLICE!
THE END?

WRITTEN BY
GREG ANDERSON-ELYSÉE

"PROLOGUE"
DRAWN & COLORED BY
LEE MILEWSKI

"FORGOTTEN STORIES"
DRAWN BY
WALTER OSTLIE
COLORED BY
LEE MILEWSKI

LETTERED BY
JOSHUA COZINE

COVER & LOGO BY
WALT MSONZA BARNA

IS'NANA
THE WERE-SPIDER

WEBWAY COMICS LOGO BY
YOSUF GURUNG

FIRST PRINTING. PRINTED IN CANADA.

BEHIND THE
SCENES

WITH ARTIST
WALTER OSTLIE

Just a warm up sketch for fun, just because these guys are hella fun to draw.

The first complete drawing of Is'nana before we had finalized his design. I remember Greg liked it, but wanted a little more muscle on the guy.

First sketches trying to find Is'nana from Greg's descriptions. This was before I had the gig and Greg wanted to see what I was all about.

Figuring out the transformation. A face only a father could love.

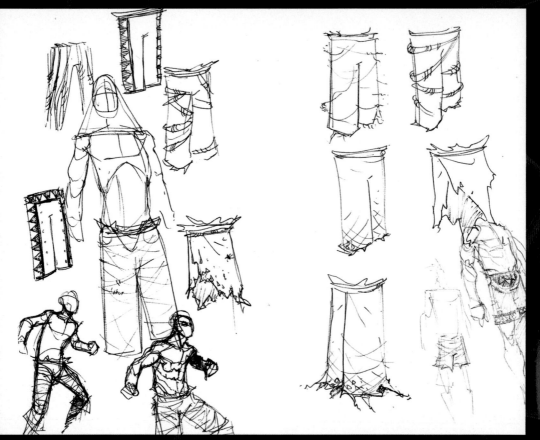

The clothes make the man and it also keeps us from having to make the book rated R. Messing around with trying to figure out how we could make his clothes look like webbing.

It's not the size, it's the proportion that matters. This was to help with the construction of the plush.

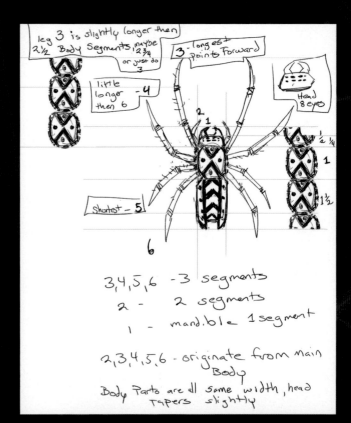

leg 3 is slightly longer then 2½ Body Segments, maybe 1 2 3/4 or just do 3

little longer — 4 then 6

3 - longest points Forward

Head 8 eyes

shortest — 5

6

½ ¼
1
1½

3,4,5,6 - 3 segments
2 - 2 segments
1 - mandible 1 segment

2,3,4,5,6 - originate from main Body

Body Parts are all same width, head tapers slightly

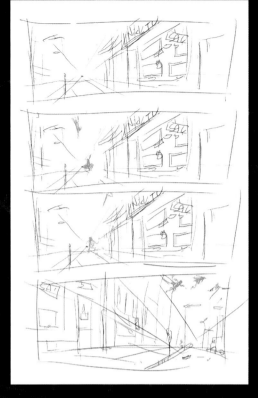

GREG: Collaboration is one of my absolute favorite things about creating and this was one of the earliest scenes I recall really going back and forth and collaborating with Walter in making this scene work. Walter didn't feel the way I had originally written the scene would work visually and had even tested it out. I try to be very open to ideas and I personally find that it makes the product a lot more fun to work on as it makes you look at things and adds nuances you didn't see prior. So we toyed further with this scene, shot ideas back and forth till we both felt it worked.

Here's how it turned out. On the next page, you can see the script for the scene as it was originally written in the first working draft. I am MUCH happier with Walter's version.

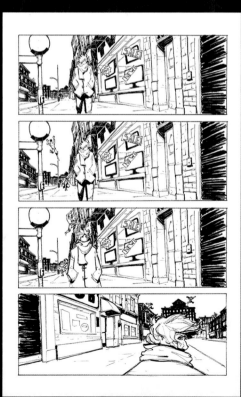

Page Six

Each of these panels I believe should be wide-panels. If another layout works better, go for it.

[Note for artist and letterer: Depending on the programs added to the other sets, I'll include "dialogue" for them. As the panels are "zooming in," the dialogue for the other programs will gradually disappear until the final panel where it's just the news report.]

Panel One:

We're outside of a television shop where there are television sets playing behind the glass windows. In the middle of the window is one particular TV showing a news report. The other TV sets can show other programs (cartoon shows, sit-coms, romance film, etc). Just make sure the middle TV set has the news program.

News Reporter: ...Autopsy reports say that the neck wounds indicate an animal attack...

Panel Two:

We're moving closer into the news programmed TV set.

News Reporter: ...the bites resembling that of a panther.

Panel Three:

We're moving closer to it. On the very right of the panel we see what may appear to be a man's leg coming into the frame. This is the first "shot" of Is'nana. He's wearing short dashiki pants. We don't see anything else of Is'nana but his legs coming into frame as he's swinging forward.

News Reporter: Investigators are attempting to inspect every zoo in the city to deduce any animals missing.

Panel Four:

We're moving in a little closer to the TV set as we see Is'nana now swinging in the middle of the frame. We shouldn't see his upper body still; we're just looking at his legs more into frame now.

News Reporter: As of today, there have been three unfortunate victims.

Panel Five:

Closer into the TV set but we see Is'nana's legs at the far left of the panel frame now, exiting. By now, this could be a full on shot on the TV screen.

News Reporter: Although an animal attack seems the likely result of these killings, investigators are not excluding human foul play...

PIN-UP GALLERY

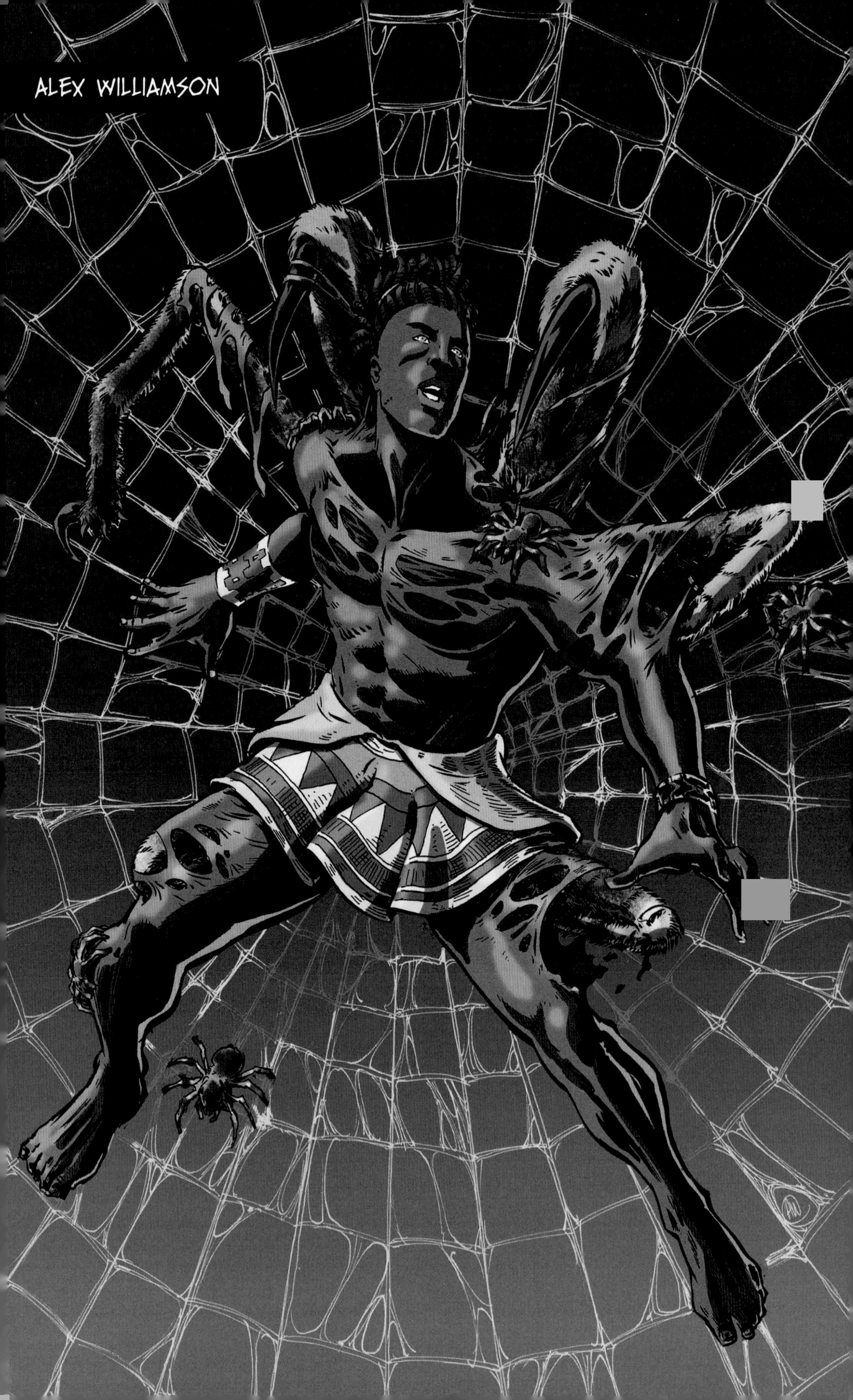
ALEX WILLIAMSON

ANTHONY GONZALES

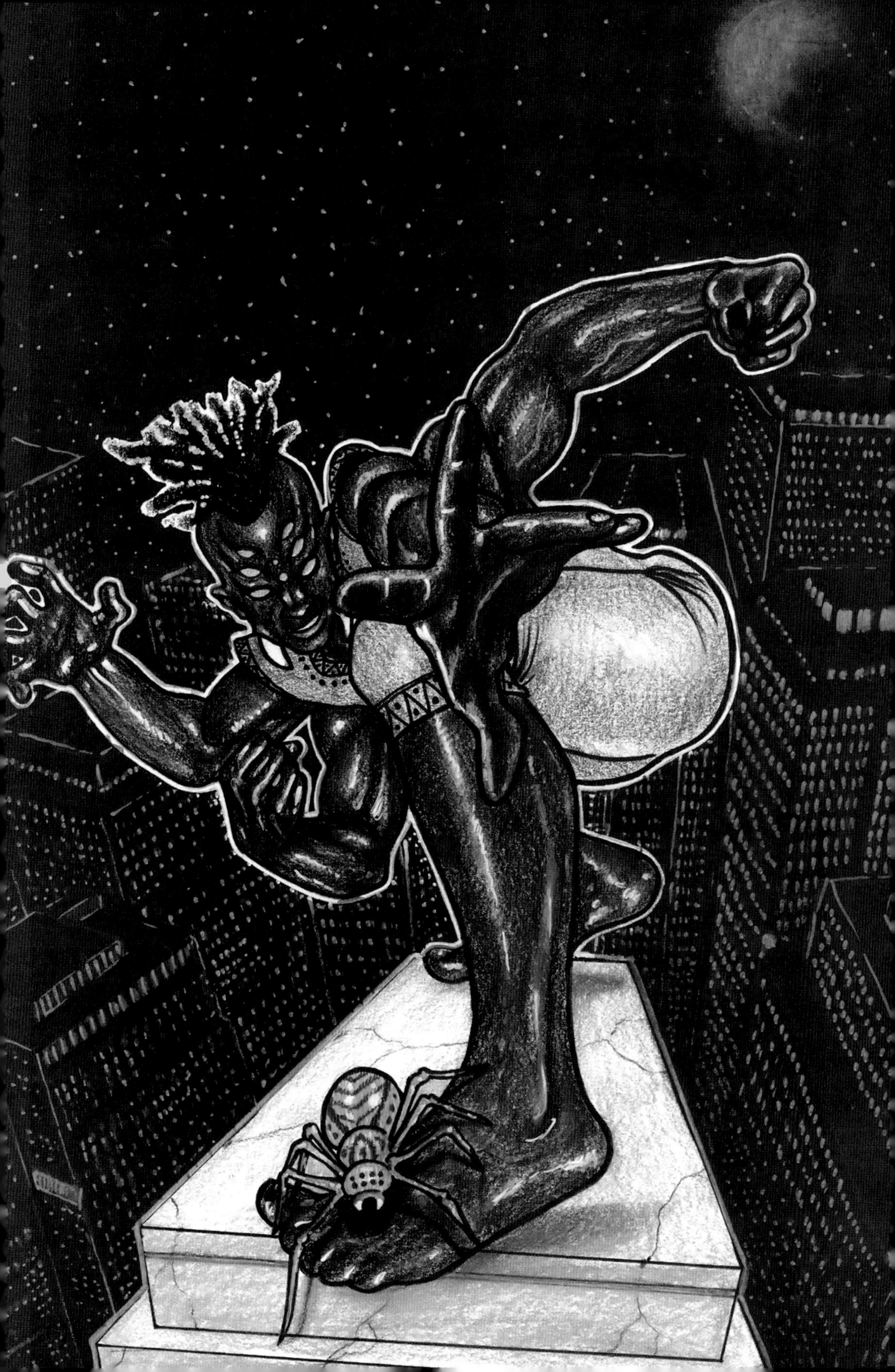

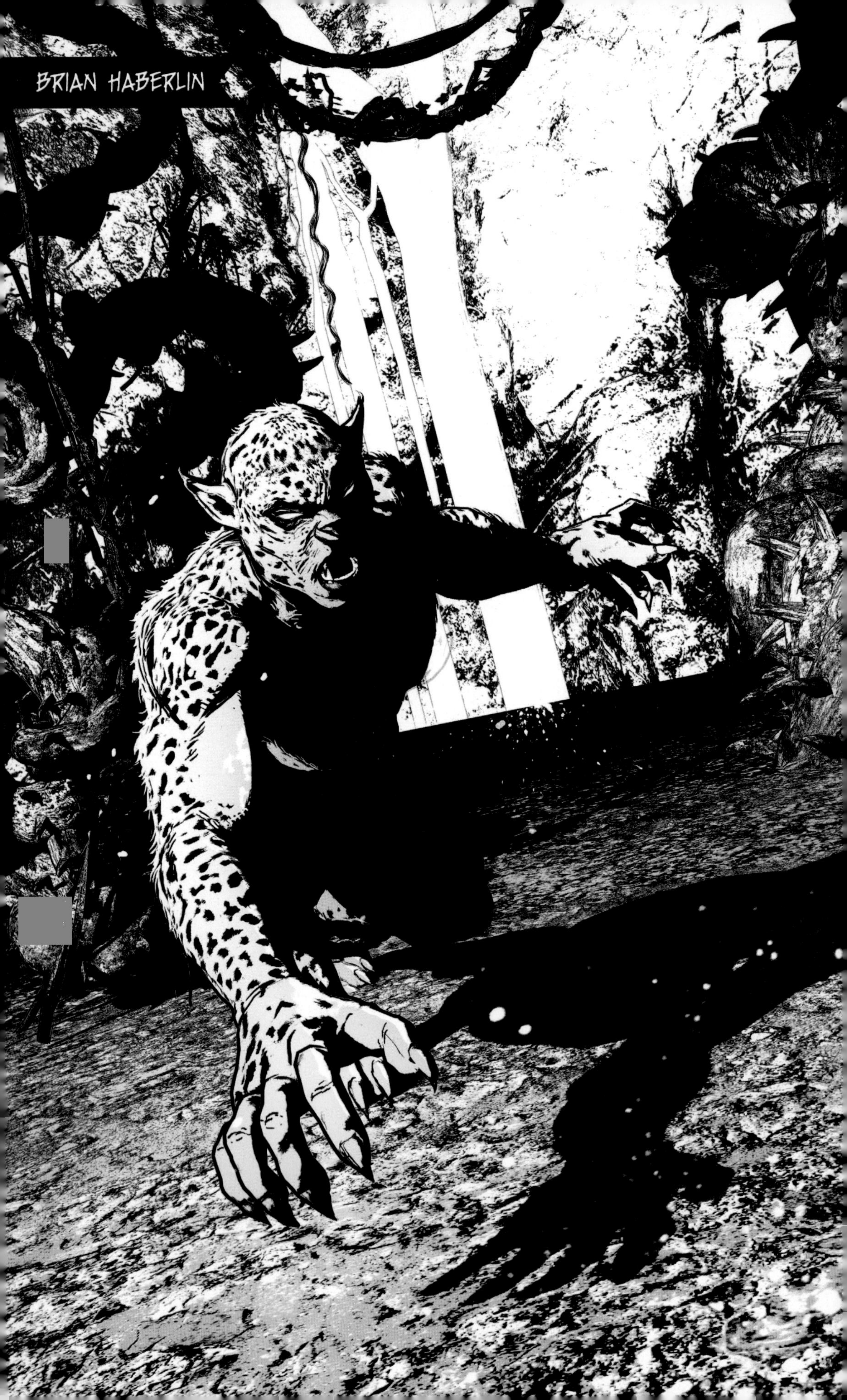
BRIAN HABERLIN

DARYL TOH

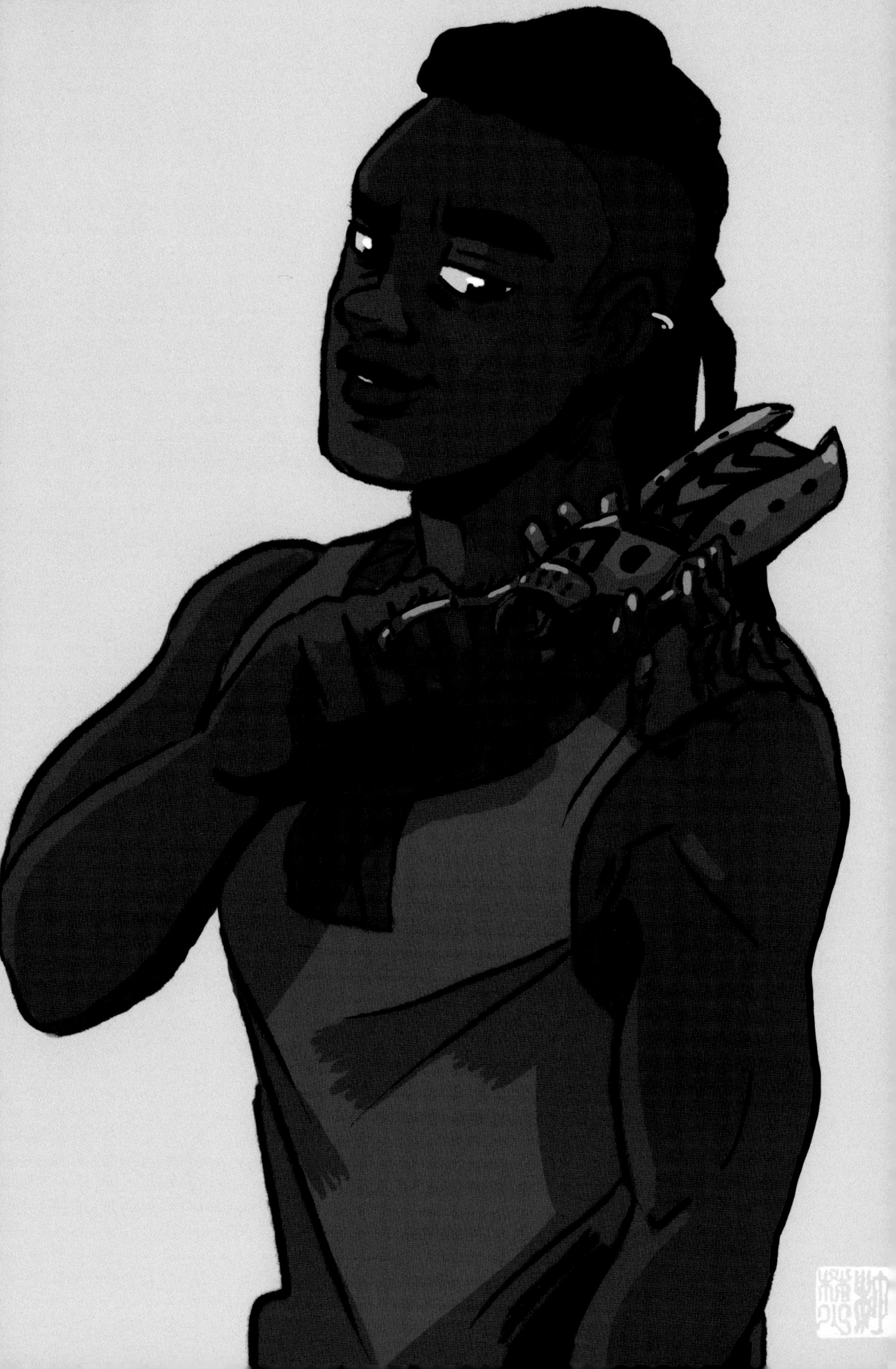

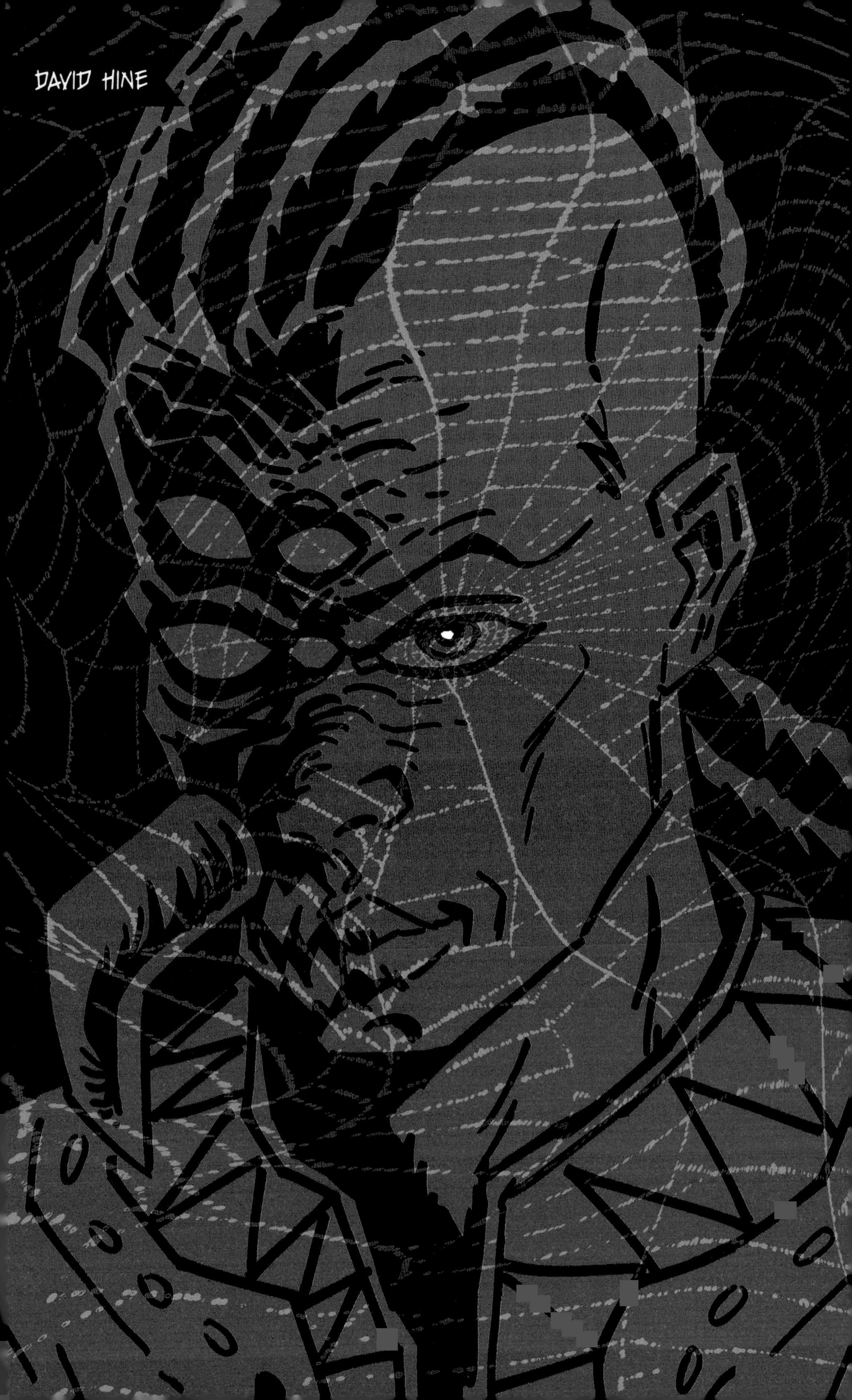
DAVID HINE

JASON REEVES

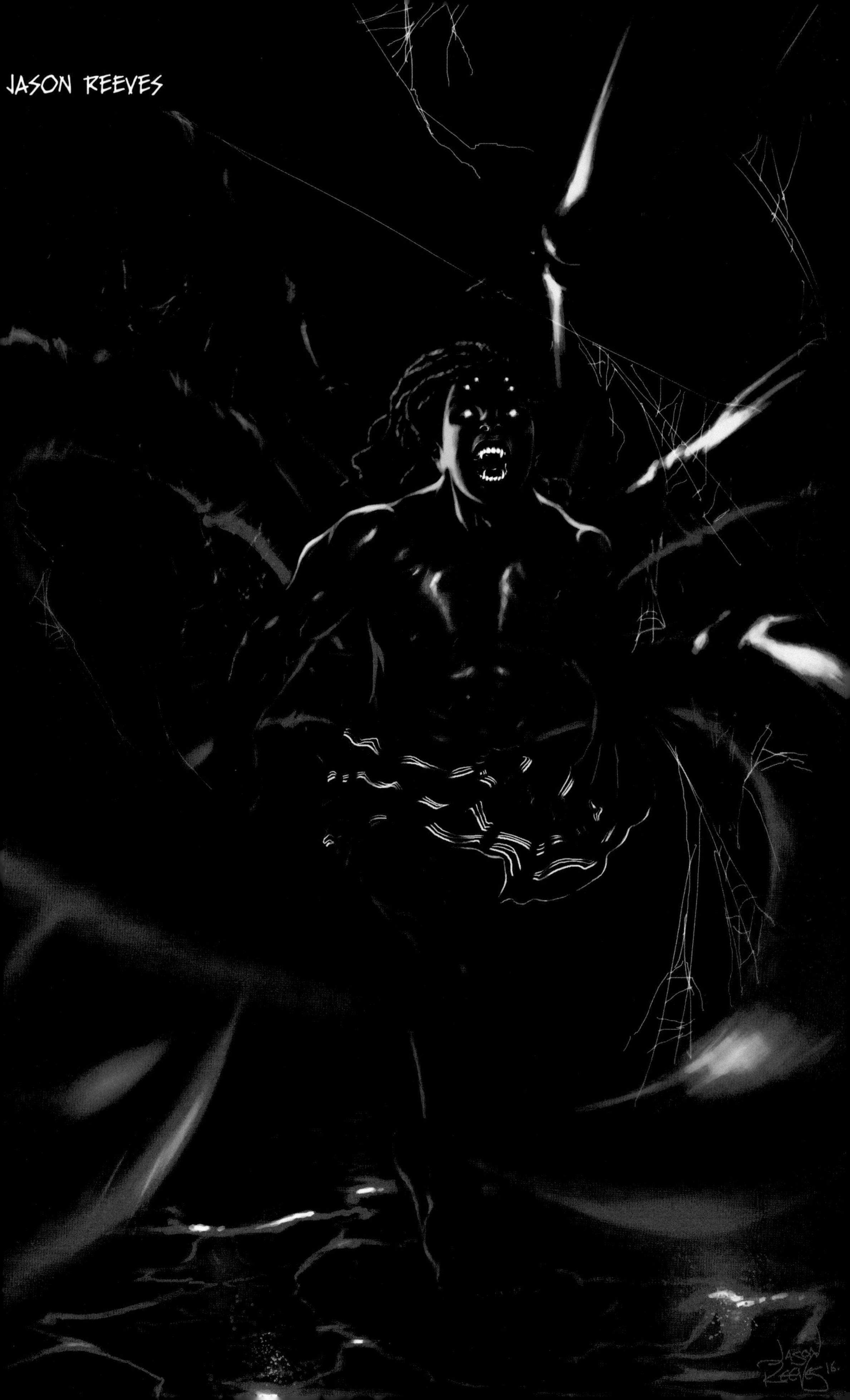
Jason Reeves 16.

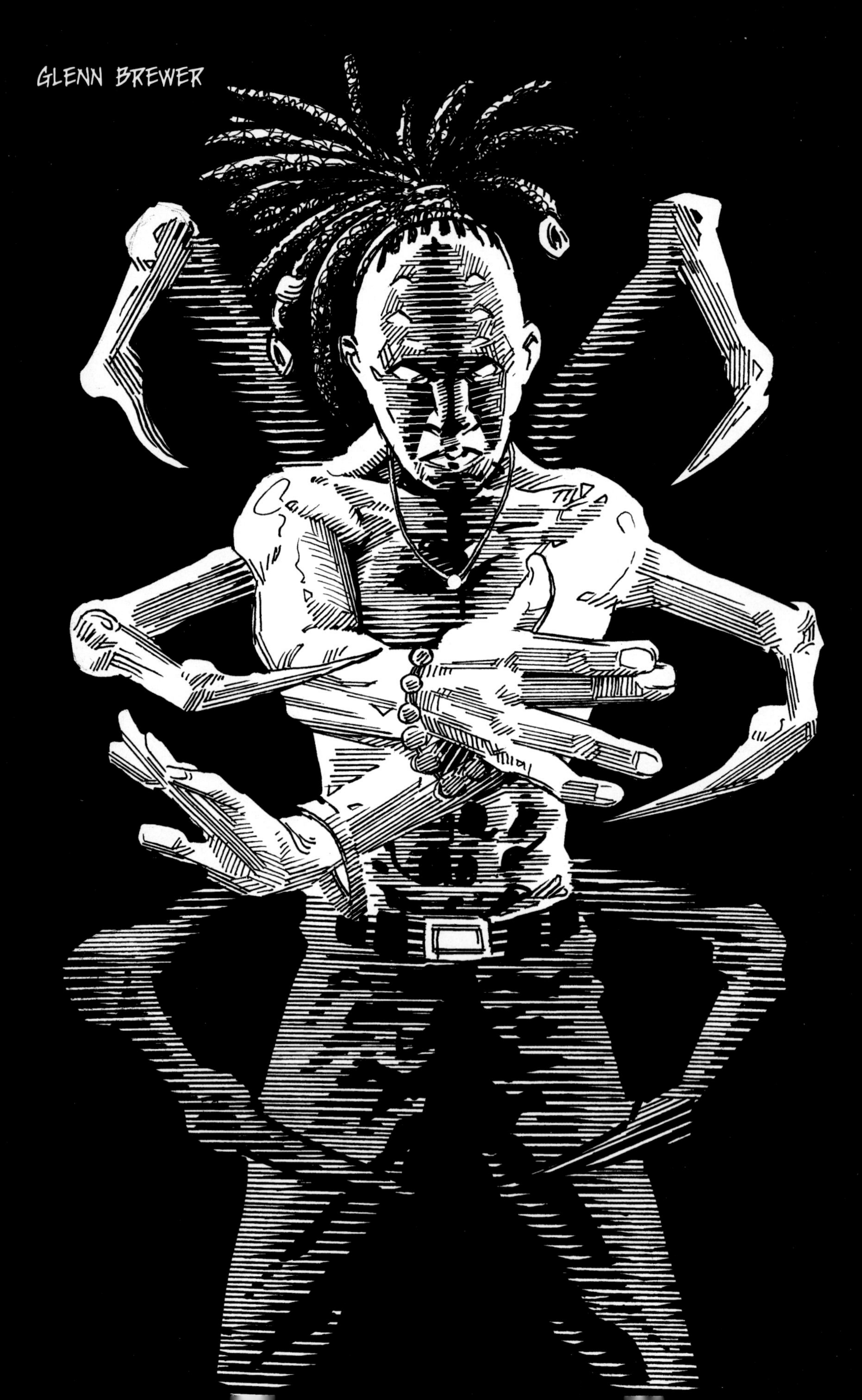
GLENN BREWER

GLENN BREWER

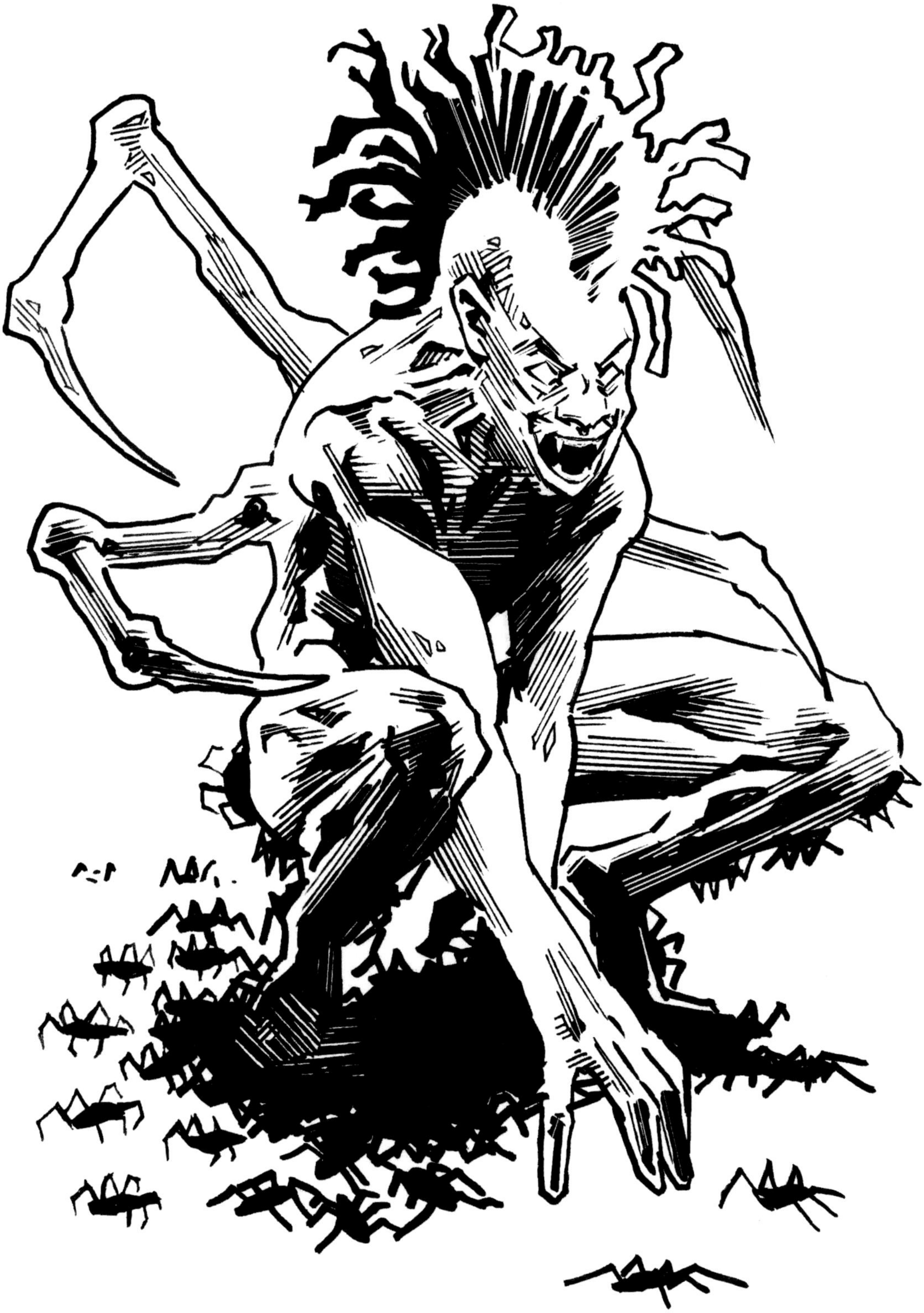

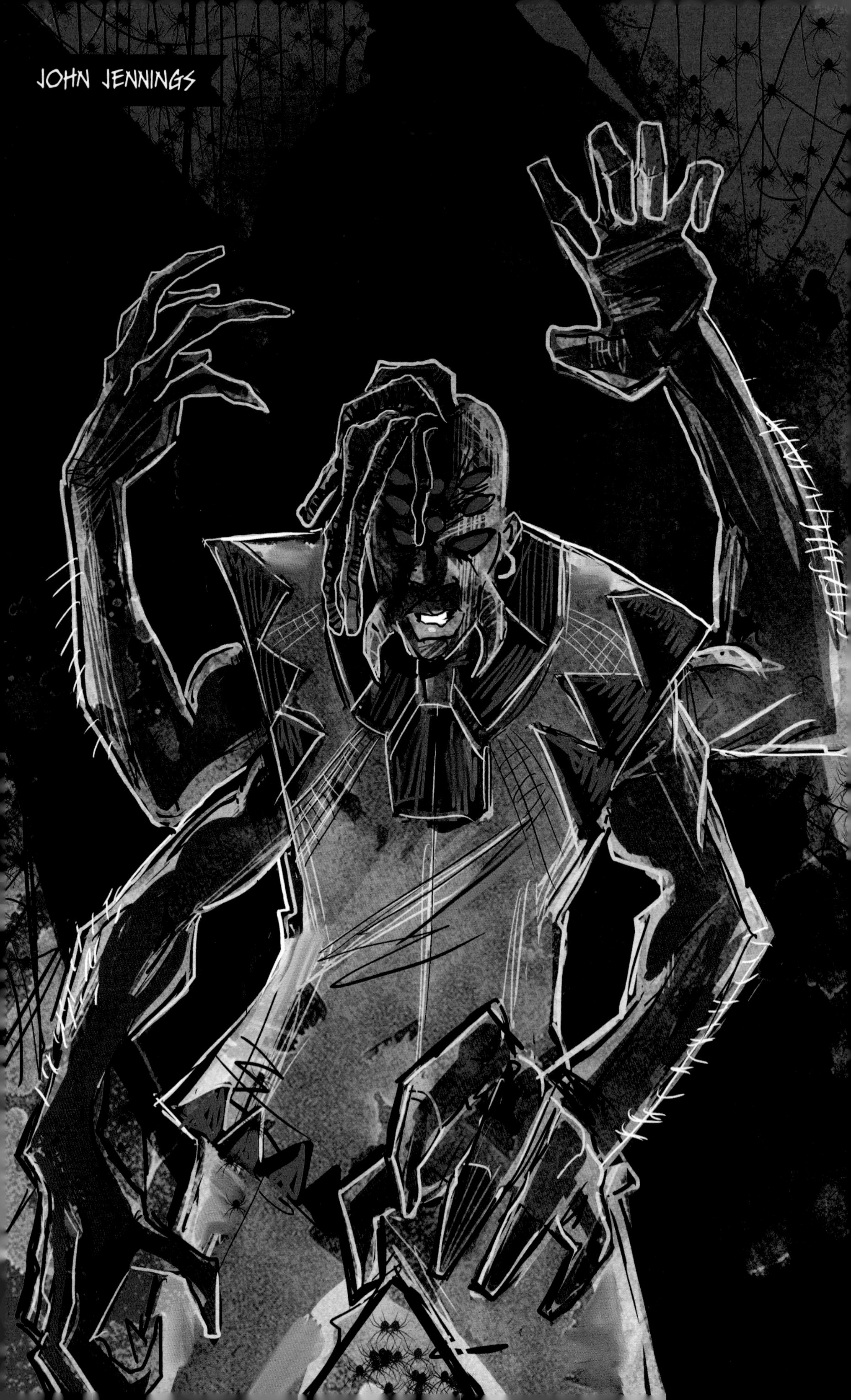
JOHN JENNINGS

KEEF CROSS

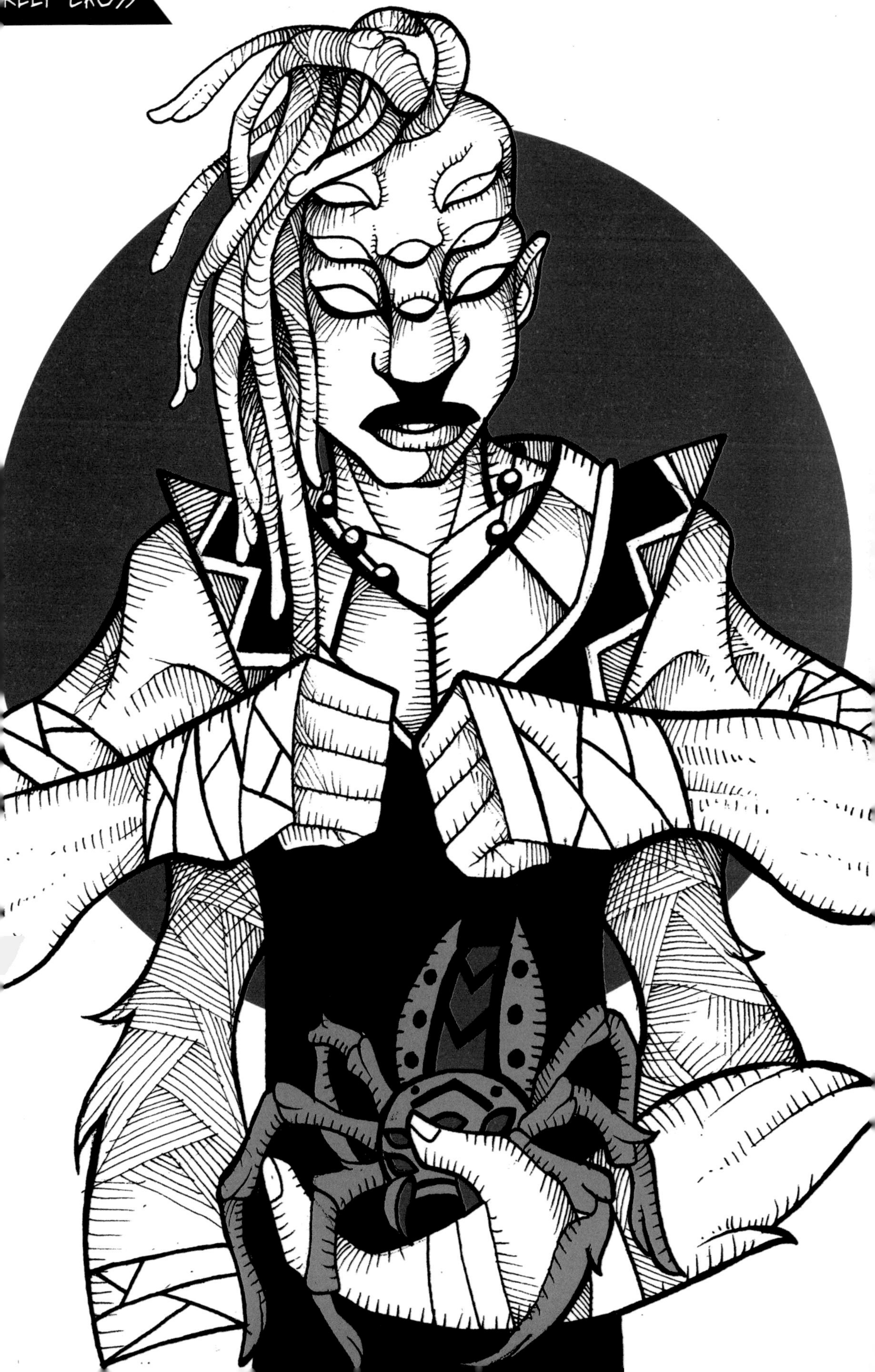

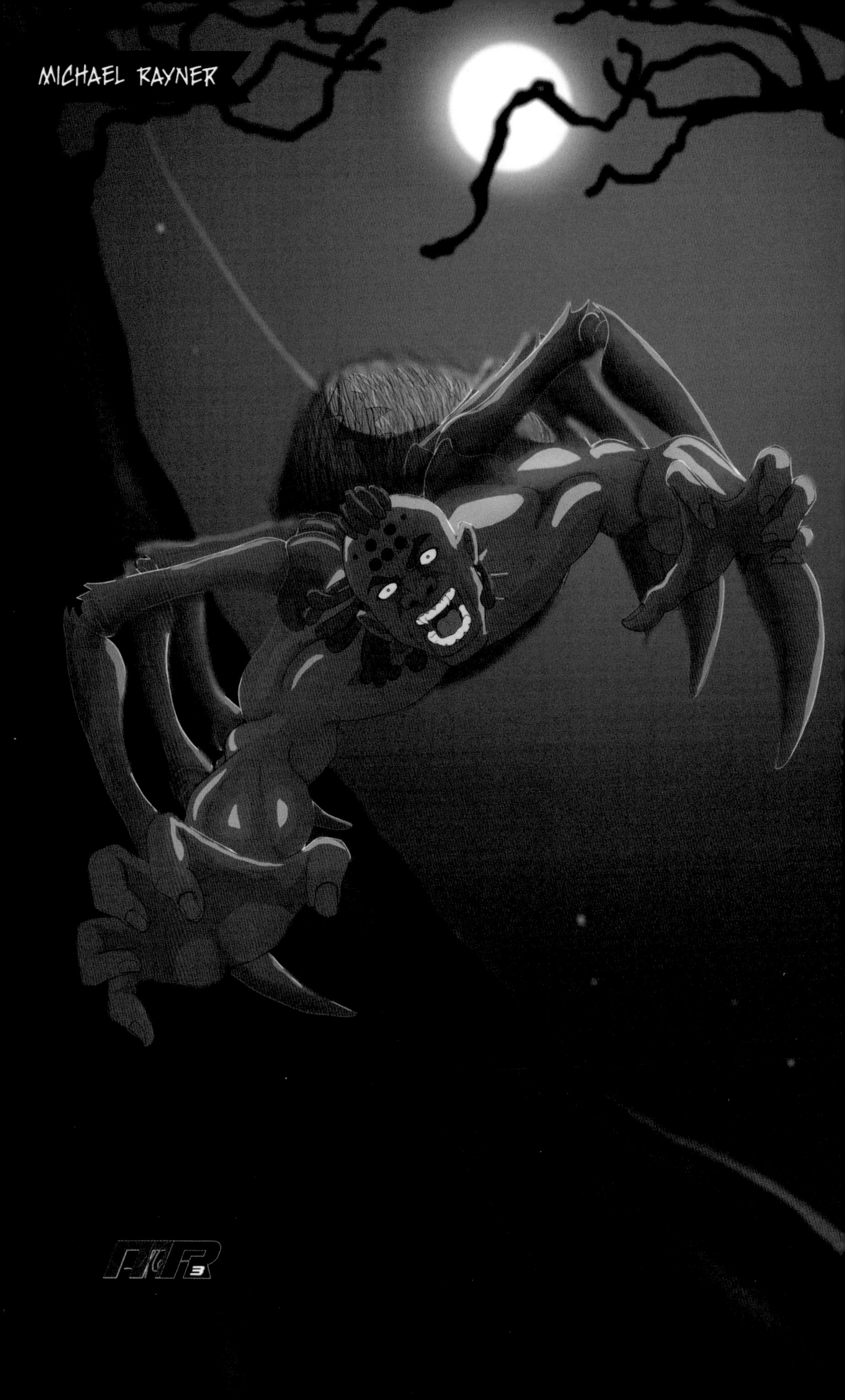
MICHAEL RAYNER

MICHAEL RAYNER

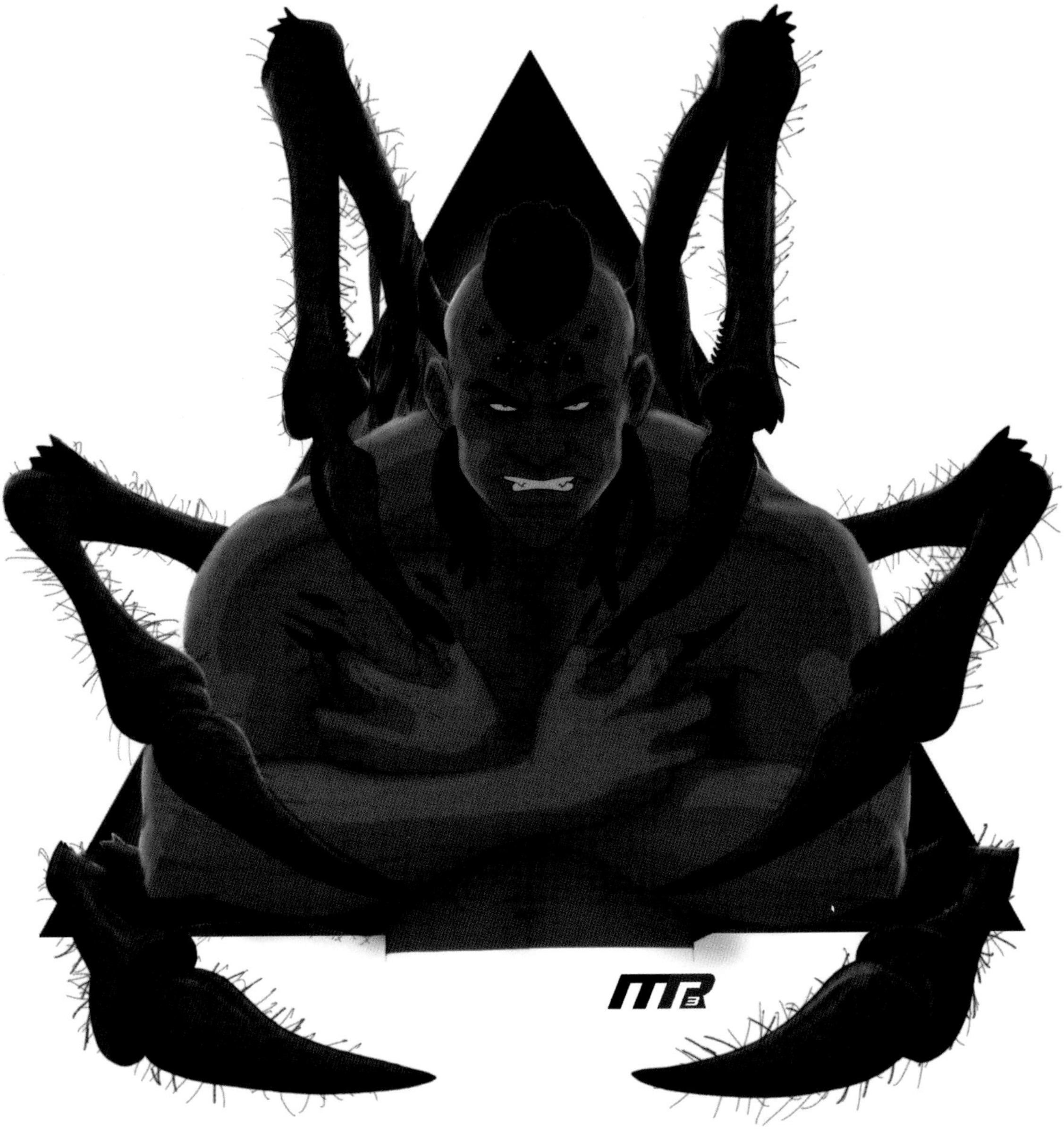

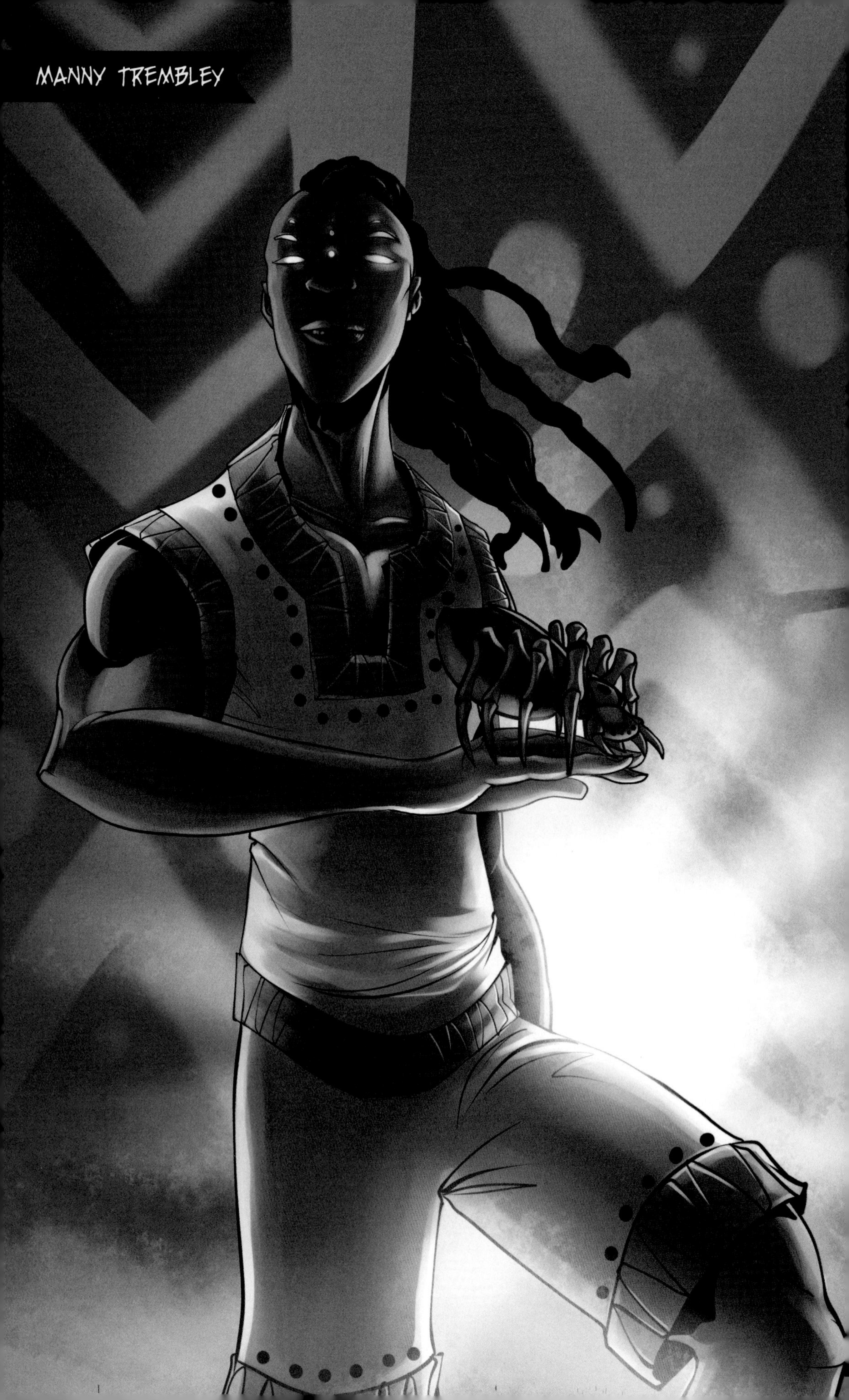
MANNY TREMBLEY

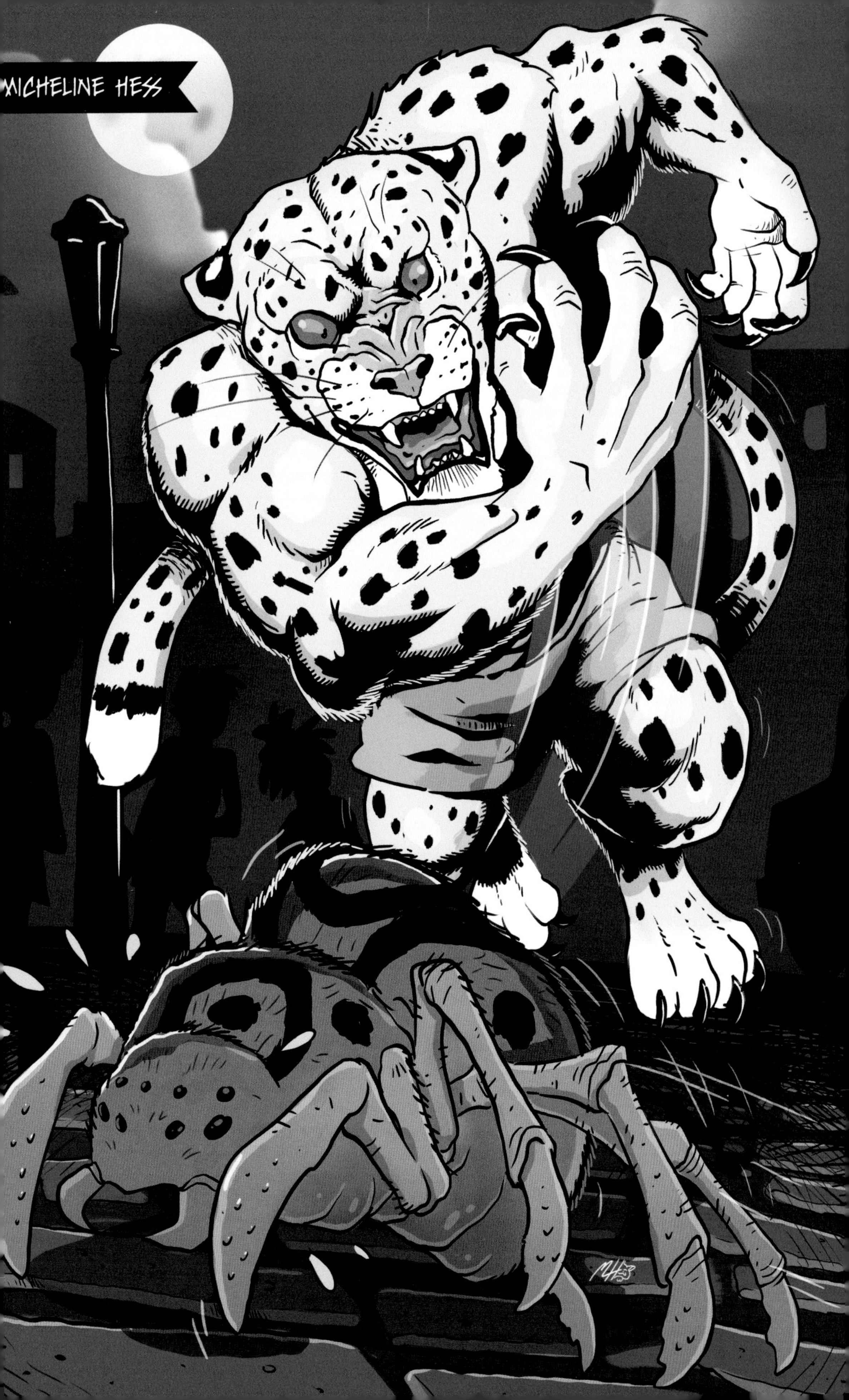
MICHELINE HESS

RAMEL HILL

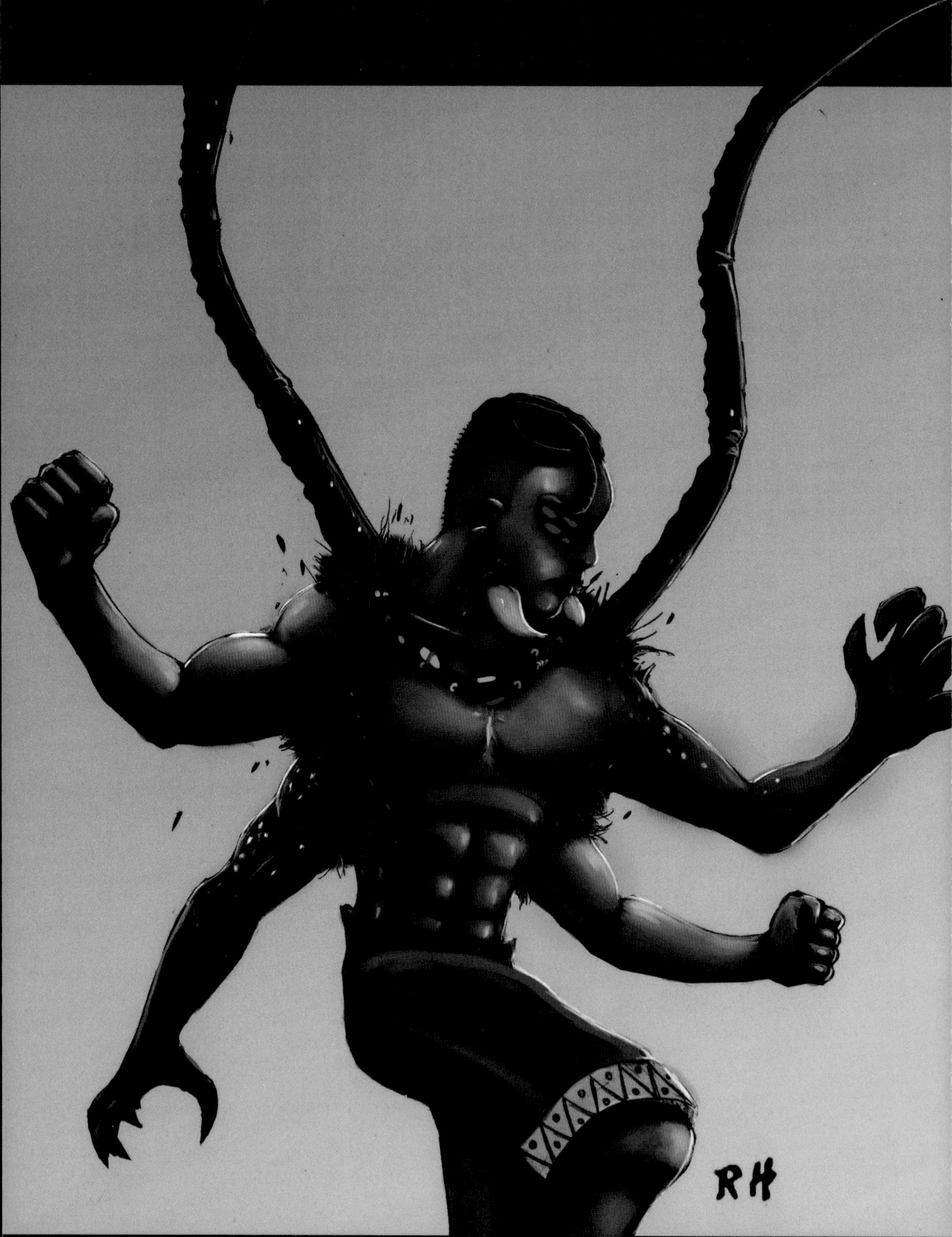
RH

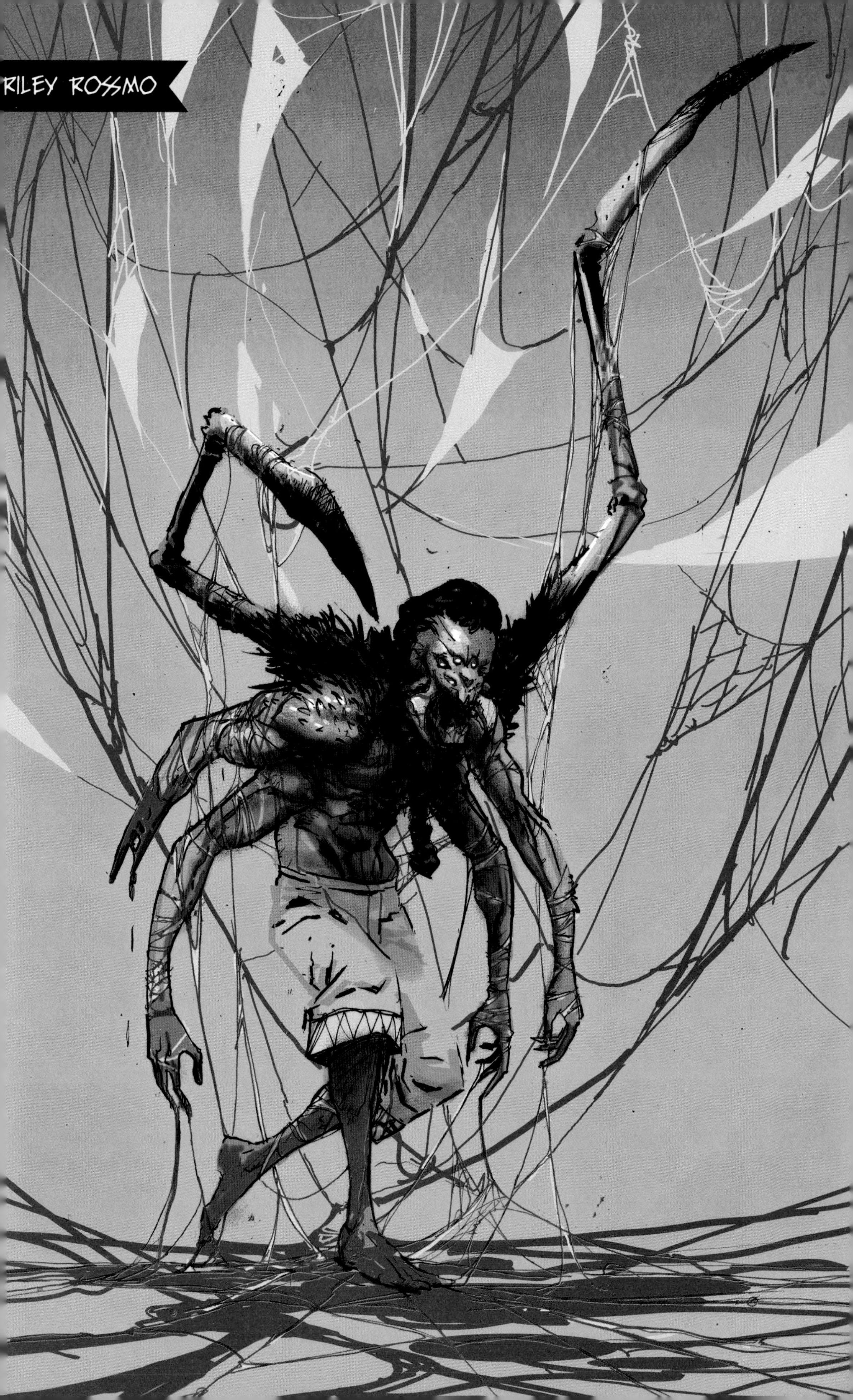

RILEY ROSSMO

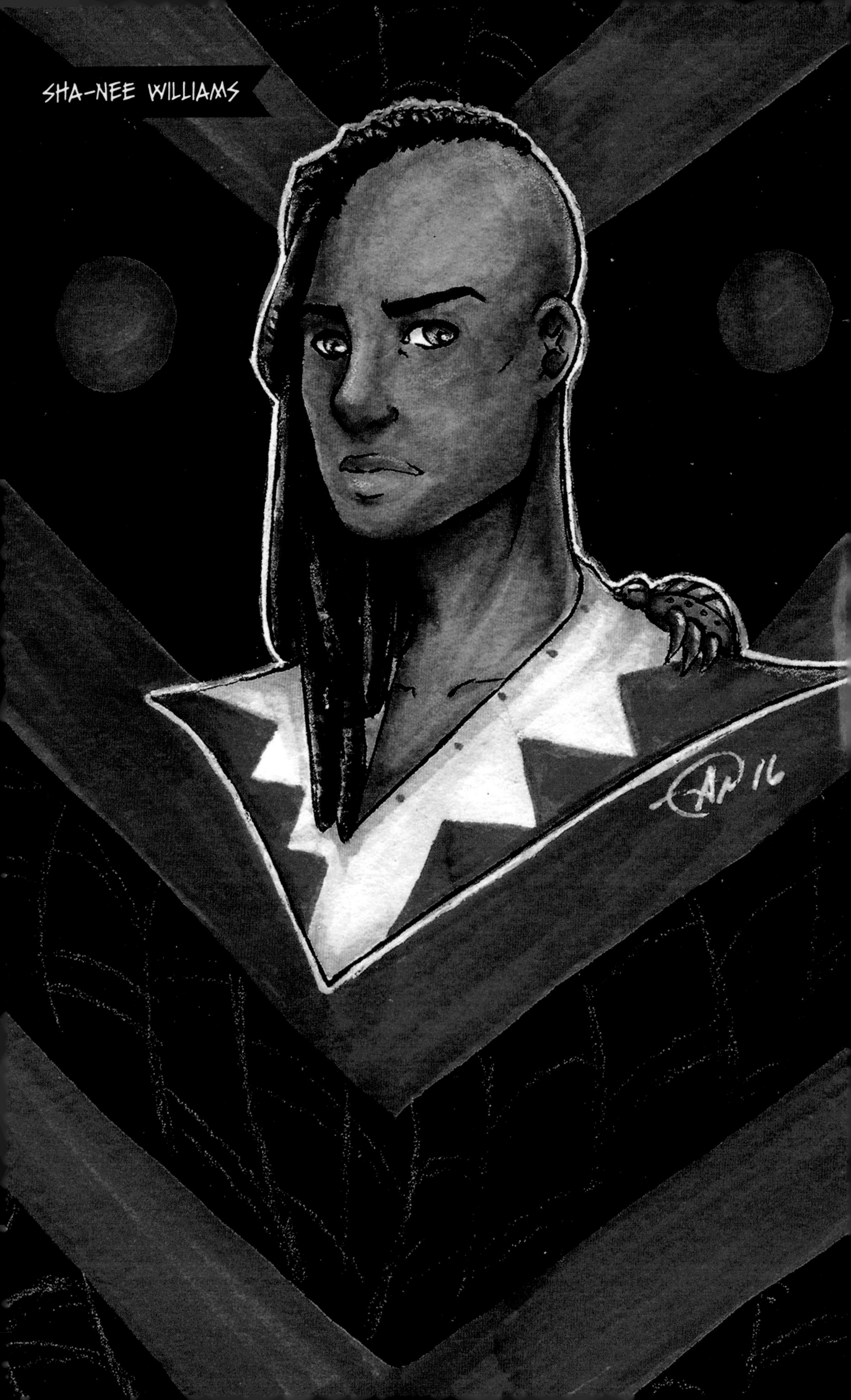
SHA-NEE WILLIAMS

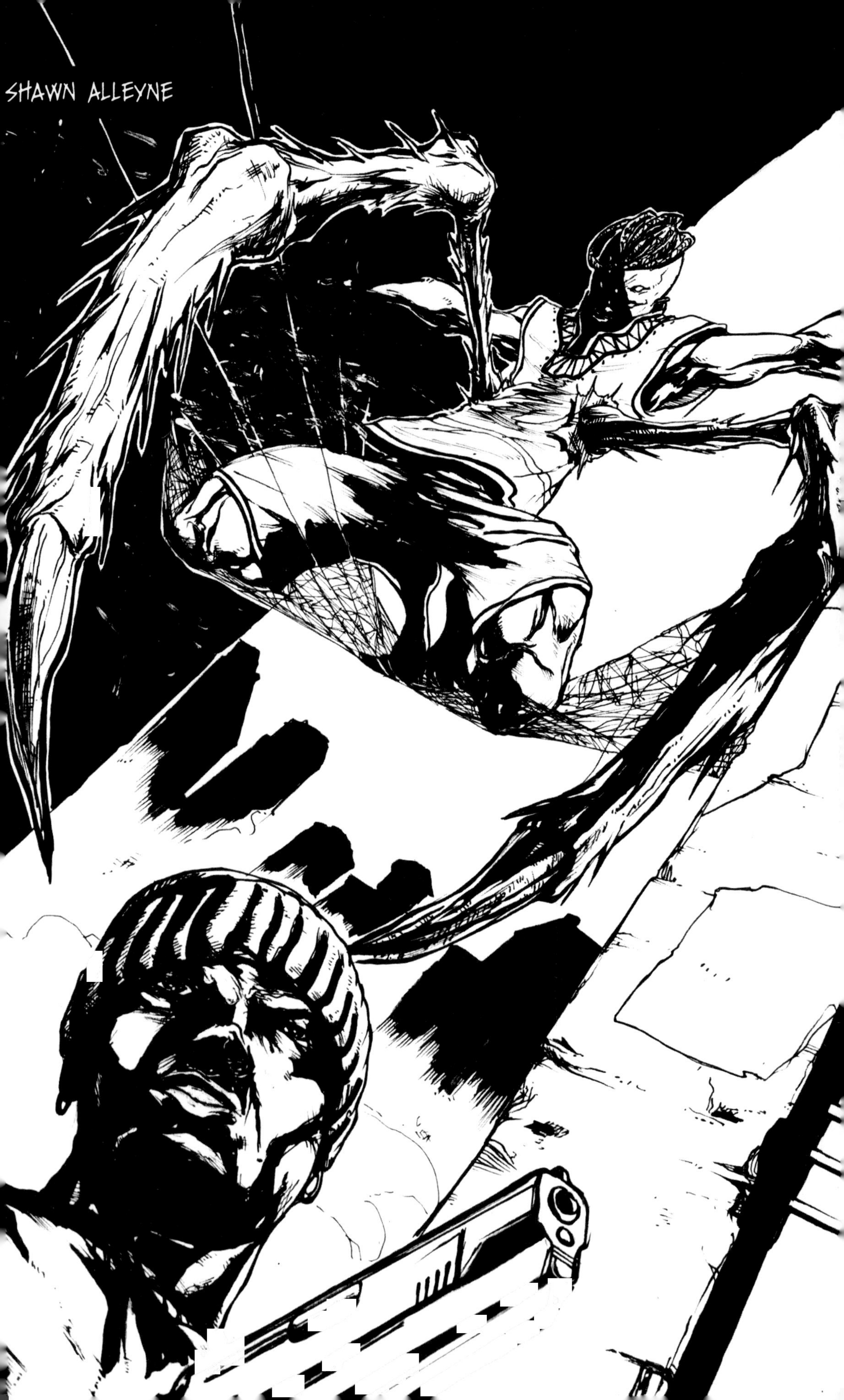
SHAWN ALLEYNE

TIM FIELDER

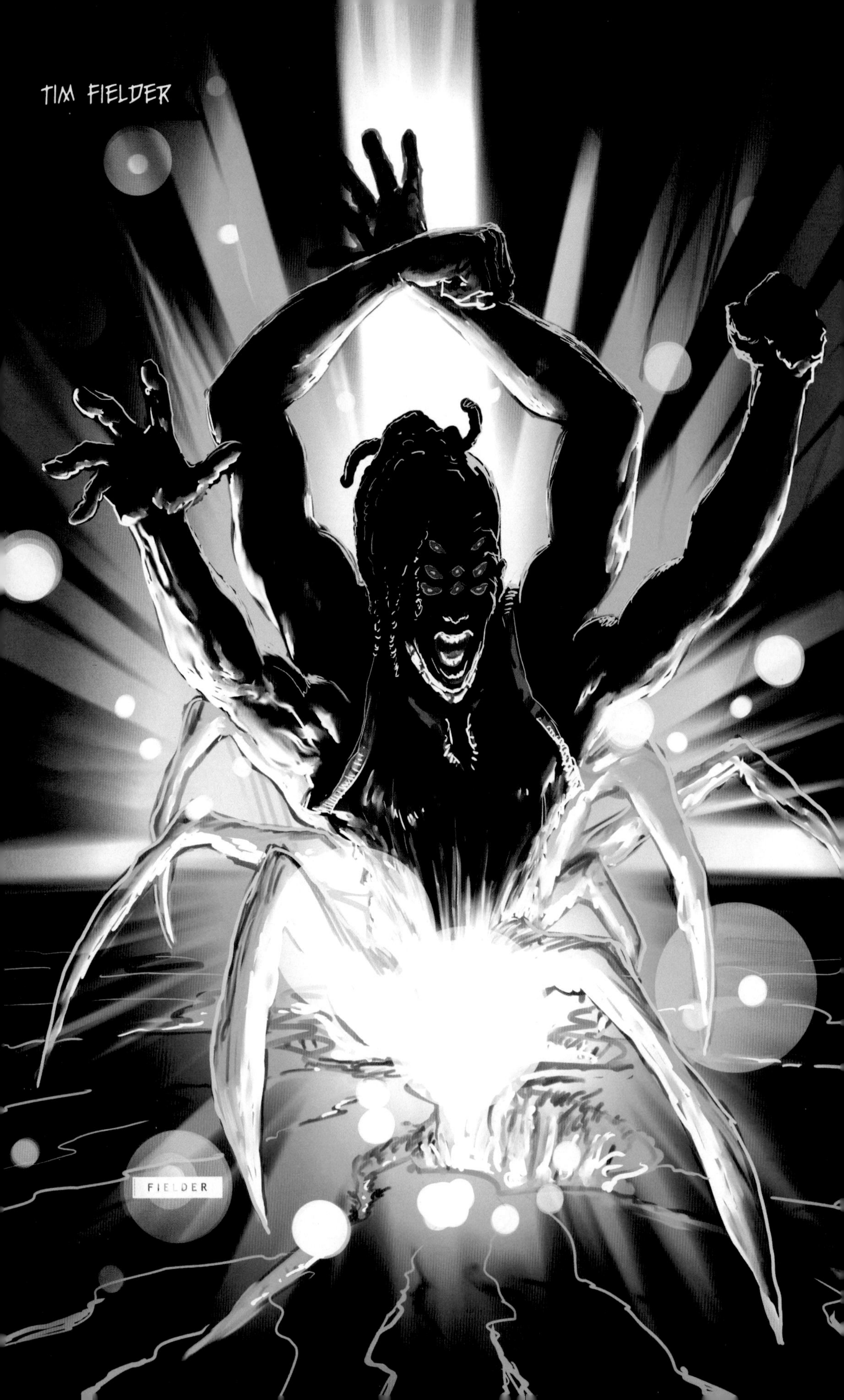
FIELDER

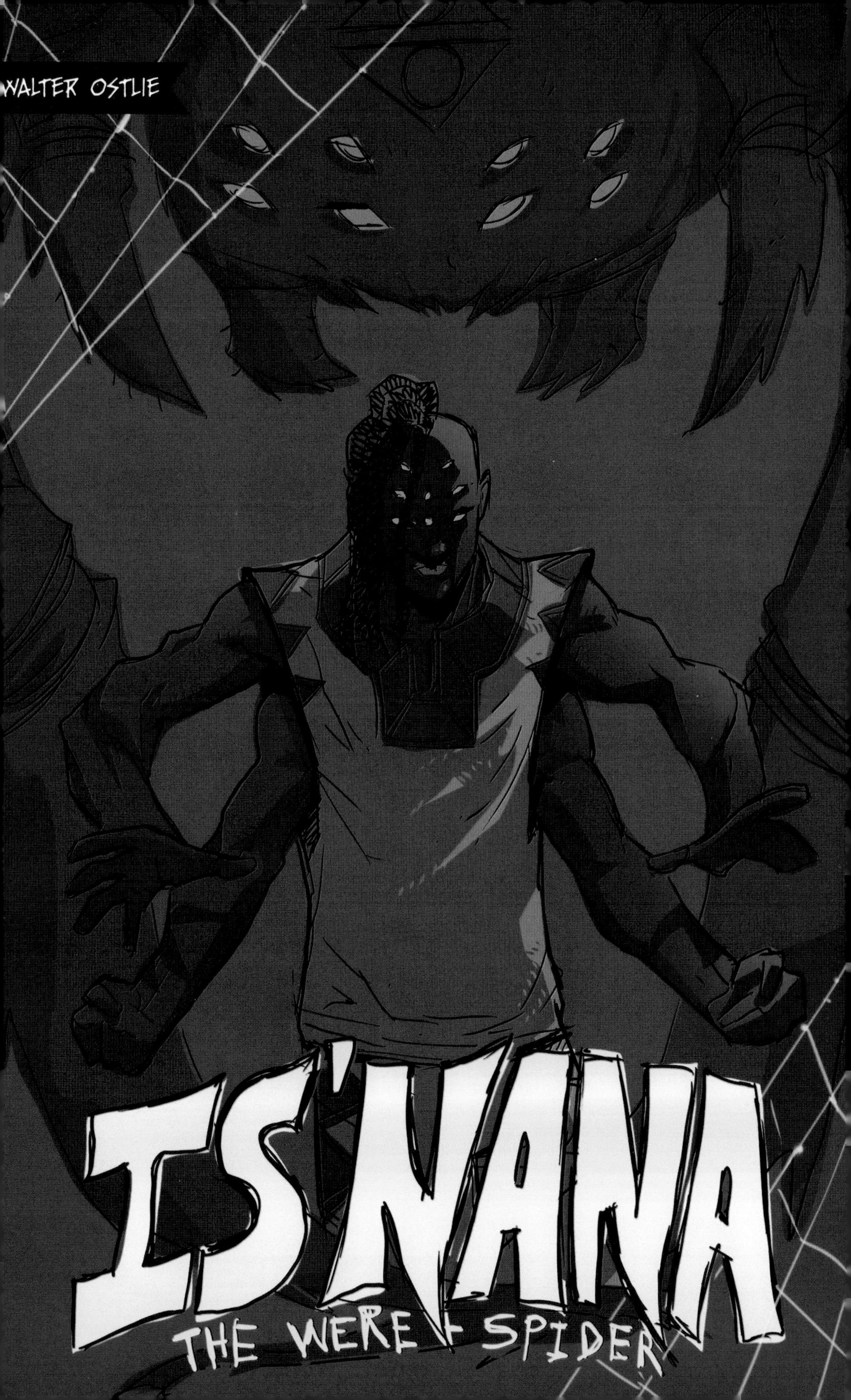
WALTER OSTLIE
IS'NANA
THE WERE-SPIDER

SCOTT BRATEK

BLAIRSULEEN MILORD

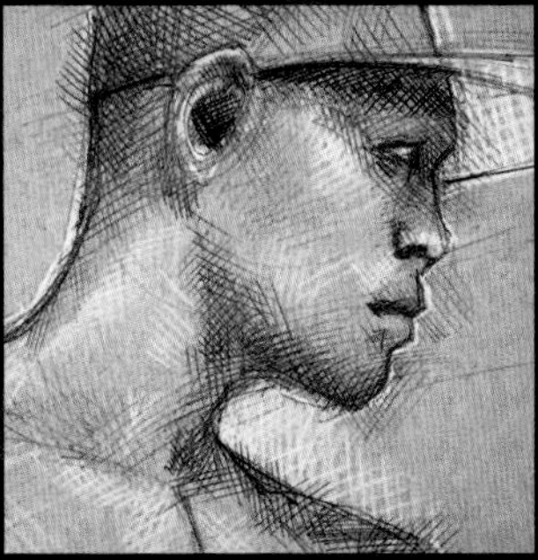

WRITER

Gregory Anderson-Elysee is a Brooklyn, NY born Haitian-American writer, film-maker, model, and teacher. He runs a column on Outhousers.com named (Heard It Thru) The Griotvine where he showcases independent creators of color and LGBTQ creators. "Is'nana: The Were-Spider" is his first comic.

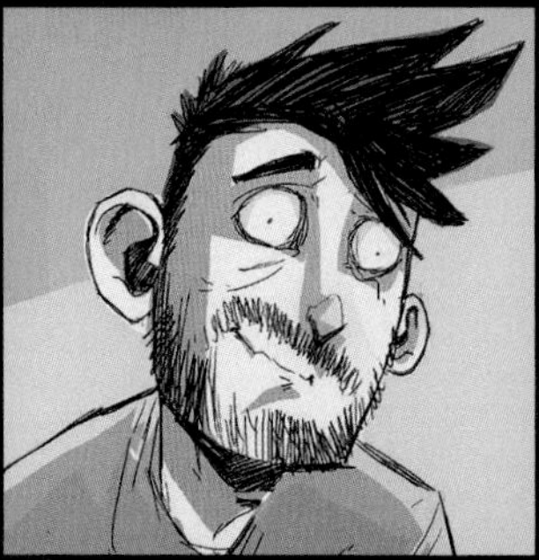

ARTIST

Walter Ostlie is a Floridian comic creator and a huge fan of creator owned content. His self-published works include "Shiver Bureau" and "Cubicles."

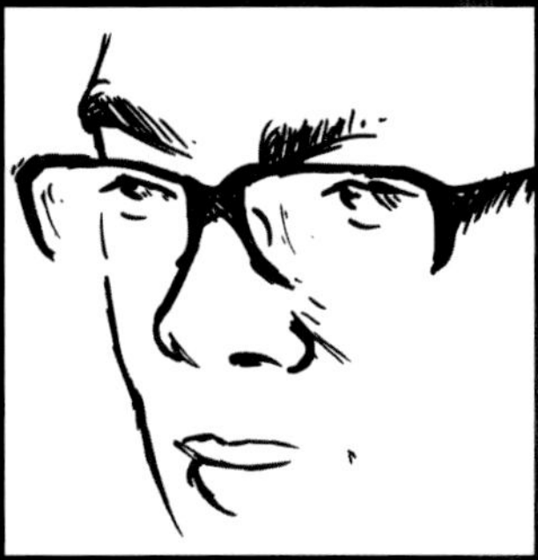

ARTIST

Lee Milewski is a professional illustrator from South West Florida, where he toils away drawing comics for himself and others. A few of the series he's illustrated and written are "Hunter's Lore" and "Focus Shift."

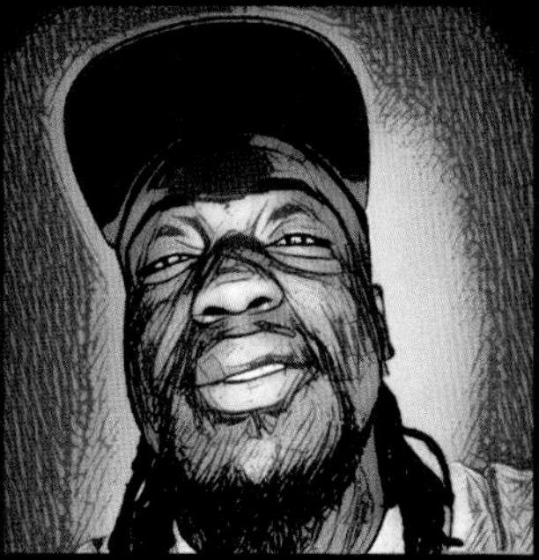

COVER ARTIST/LOGO DESIGNER

Walt Msonza Barna is a Zimbabwean freelance illustrator residing in Cape Town, South Africa. He has illustrated/co-created numerous books including "The Dark Foundations"

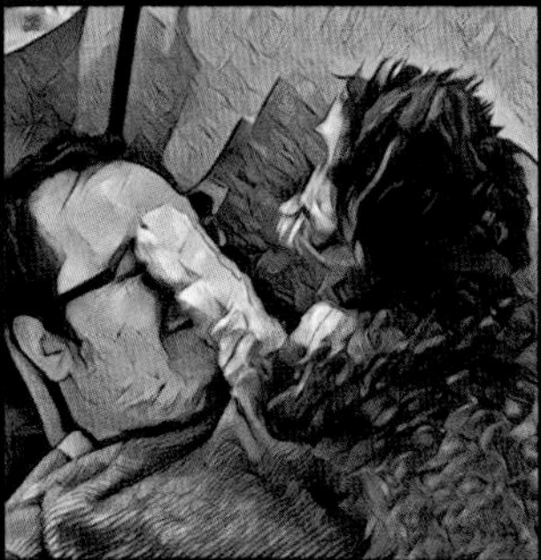

LETTERER/DESIGNER

Joshua Cozine is a jack of all trades in the comic industry. He has put words in the mouths of Batman, Superman, and The Six Million Dollar Man, which impressed the Hell out of his inner child.

SPECIAL THANKS TO:

Daniel Elysee (Thank you, Dad!!) - Marvin Gordon - Bertolain Elysee - All of my family for their continuing love and support - My mentor David Hine - Shaun Seneviratne - Anthony McPherson - Joe Dulude II - Dante Jayce - Ishmael Levi - Molevson Felican - Larry Underwood

THANK YOU TO ALL MY KICKSTARTER PLEDGERS:

@breshnyda - @ovenland - Avon - 133art - Aaron Coutee - Aaron T - Akariel Ford - Akil Harris - Alan Cohen - Alec Benoit - Alex Bates - Alexander Carey - Alexander "Guddha" Gudenau -Alexander Wright - Alioscia - Alix B - Allan & Joseph Bennington-Castro - Andre Nedderman - Andre Reynolds - Andreas Larsson - Andrew Biviano Dinges - Andrew Guilde - Andrew Whelan - Andy T - Andy Erickson - Angel E. Hardy - Angeline C Burton - Anne-Marie Kirwan - Anonymous - Anthony Christou - Anthony McClung - Anthony Miller - Anthony Piper - Araselle - Ashleigh Davenport - Ashley Geoghegan - Ashley Holmes - Ashley R. Johnson - Asmus Birch Jensen - Augie March - Ayanni C. Hanna - Balda - Ben & Ryn - Benjamin Hale - Bill Campbell - billkarson - Blanks! - Brandon Thomas - BrentP - Brenton Poke - Brian Haberlin - Brian Kieffer - Brian & Anne Gray - Brittany Wilbert - Bryan Campbell - Byron Emerson - C.R. Ward - Caitlin Jane Hughes - Caitlin MacKay Shaw - Caleb Palmquist - Cam Dow - Carl Rigney - Carlos Ors - Carlos M. - Cayden Jobson-Hawthorne & Tristan Chamberlayne - Cecil Rijken - Cecil Kidenda - Chad LeClaire - Cheslan Simpson - Chris Antony - Chris Bishop - Chris Buchner - Christina Major - Christina - Christopher Kettle-Frisby - Christopher Wright - Chuck "Rooster" Bonakoski - Cindy Womack - Claire E. Gill - Colton Nyegaard - Cory Puga - Crystal O'Rourke - Cynthia McDonald - D.A. Dryden - Dain Eaton - Damian Hinks - Dan O'Callaghan - Dane Cardiel - Daniel Brodie - Daniyil Yasharal - Dan Loyd + Fiona Ferguson-Loyd - Dajomu - Daniel Stalter - Danielle Eden - David Accampo - Dave Krawchuk - David Krouse - David Mortman - Dean Simons - Deja Hodg - aka Varah - Denis Lasana - Dennis Strasburg - Derek Tobler - Devon Camel - Devon Tabris - Dr DeVonte Lamont Glass - Diana Green - Dianna Anthony & David Dawson - Dirk W. - Domenick Pontoriero - Dwayne Simon - Dylan - Echo Mae - Ed Moore Jr. - Eder Silva - Edward R. Booker - Elaine - Emilie Nicole Hanson - Emilie Dion - Enrique Carrion - Eric Damon Walters - Eric Ivan Garcia - Eric Ratcliffe - E. Outley - Eric Piñero - Erik T Johnson - Erin Shade - Erin Subramanian - Errol Lobo - Faina Gordover - Faith Roncoroni - Farley Samson - Ferdinand von Schenk - Fleur Mongan - FotD Team - Frank Jaeger - Frankie Mundens - G Boney - Gabriel Pacheco - Gary Ross - Gheru - Grant Collins - Greg and Fake - Greg Burnham - Greg Randolph - Greg "schmegs" Schwartz - Grizzly Forged Studios, LLC - Guy Copes - Harvey Carlson - Harvey Redding - Hillary Graham - Hollow Mask - Horace Mandroid - Huang - Hue Reviews - InnHuchen - Isaiah Coleman - Inara -Iva & Rogan - J. Miles Dunn - Jackie Chang - Jacques Nyemb - Jamal - Jamal Atiq Howard - James E. Roche - James Haick - James S. Skala, Jr. - Jamie R. Van Doren - James - Jan Chan - Jann Kuosa - Keiji Miashin - Jason Brown - Jason Graoroski - Jason Hurst - Jason Jackson - Jason Stone - Jay Lofstead - Jef Zwirek - Jen Klaus - Jenny Mure - Jeremy Zimmerman - J. Tulio - Jesse Morgan - Jesse McGowan - Jessica McBee - J.L. Wheeler-Diggs - Joan Johnson - Joane - Joe Hilliard - Joe Illidge - John T. - John Rooster Ford - John L. Vogt - John Lawson - John MacLeod - John Murphy - John M. Shoestock Jr. - The Awesome J.M. Hunter - Jonas and Nicole Soderstrom - Jonathan Shaver - Jordan Lisi - Jose Pagan - Josh Rose - Josh Alan Doetsch - Joshua Albert Sinsel - Josh Gregoire - Joshua "Yolkum" Janes - Jovan Lopez de Victoria - Jragon S - Jule Bristow - Juliana Lai - Julie Phillips - Justin Alexis - Justin Bolger - Justice Family - Kariane Lemay - Karl Blue Robinson - Katie Dalby - K.C. Anderson - Keith Borgholthaus - Keiji Miashin - Kenna Thom - Kenneth A Brown - Kenneth Stickland - Kerwin Warneke - Kevin Cuffe - Kevin J. "Womzilla" Maroney - Kevin Joseph - Kevin Wellman - Killian Boyd - Kirk Johnson - Kori Flint - Korinne Martin - Lemar Williams - Lance - Larry Fullmore Jr. - Laura A. Burns - Laura Rushing - Lauren Alexandria - Lawrence Norman - Lee-David Watson - Lennox Family - Leon & Theo - Lila Green - Lissette Evans - LivingWine - Liz - Logan - Lou Casey - Luke Spoon - MacawEagle - Maggie Tagoe - Malcolm Lee - Manny Trembley - Marcus Cox - Marcus A. - Marc André Laurence - Margaret St. John - Marilyn Donahue - Mark Chapman - Mark H. Porterfield - Mark Tanriku - Martin Arroyo - Martin DeRiso - Martin E. Stein - Mary Jane Lloyd - Marygrace Burns - Mathias Pletschacher - Matt (Twpsyn) Hill - Matt Sanders - Matt Townsend - Meaghan Morrison - Megan "M5" Matta - Melissa Johnson - Melissa McGee - Michael Bukraba - Michael Elliott - Michael J. Ruiz-Unger - Michael "Bowtie" Muske - Michael Orvis - Michael Rolleri - Michael Suzio - Michail Dim. Drakomathioulakis - Michelle M. Pessoa - Midwest Ethnic Convention For Comics And Arts (MECCAcon) - Miguel Angel Perez - Mike "MFANARTIST" Colston - Mike & Jen Vance - Mike Whooley - Milton Benn - Mindy Weisberger - Miranda Dees - Montrell Marshall - Molly O'Connell - Mychal Willis - N. Steven Harris - Nam Nguyen - Narjes Ruyan - Nathan Heigert - Nathaniel S. Venzor - Mark R. Lesniewski - Neil Aristy - Nelson - Nelson Cheney - Nia Imani Scott - Nick That Weird Gecko - Guy Esposito - Nick Fin - Nicole LoMauro - Nikki Michell - NY - Okwudili Udeh - Olivier Vergnault - Omar Kooheji & Annabel Campbell - Owen John Ryan - Paisley Green - Paradox Girl - Patrick Birtles - Patrick Cahn - Patrick Jao - Patrick Sessoms - Patrick Jao - Paul B. Savage - Peggy - Perry Clark - Peter Luangrath - Pharoah Bolding - Pip - POV Comics - Praveen Sawh - Qaantar - Oliver C. - Rachel Sumaray - Robert Smith - Rafa Reyes - Rafael Torres Lopez - Ralph - Rame Rocket-Man Hill - Ramon van Alteren - Dr. Randy Raghoonanan - Raquel Orozco - Ray Bonderer - Ren Rodriguez - Rhel ná DecVandé - Richard Beeby - Richard 'Mad Maru' Rochester - Richard M. Hopple, Jr. - Ricky Ribeiro - Rob Ryan - Robert Monroe, Jr. - Robert Reed - Robin B - Rodney Thomas - Rohel Terrazas - Roisin McCormac - Ronald L. Stevens, Jr. - Rory - Rory M. Christian - Ross Theriault - Roye Okupe - Rust Fox - Ryann Streicher - R~ - Sarah Kellman - Scot Myers - Scott Bratek - Scott Foy - Scott Petersen - Scot Roche - Sean Hopkins - Sean Malone - Sean R. Scott - Seantiel Way - Sebastian Hummel - Serena K. Sergey Anikushin - Sergio Hernández - Seth Morris - Sha-Née Williams - Shakirah M Bourne - Shannon Milayna Huber - Shannon Perry - Shaun Hastings - Shawn Alleyne - Shawn P. Ausherman - Shelby aka Marvelfreak - Sincere Ignorance - P. Macuda - Soraya Hawes - Spongefile - Stan Styles - Stefan K. Scheid - Stefan immerstatter - Stefani Saintonge - Stephen Rose - Stephen Thomas Bayley - Steve Tanner - Steven Danielson - Stuart Rothwell - Sue Kofi - Sumon Saha - Susan Livingston & David Nichols - Suzene Campos - Sven of the Dead - Sylvia B. - Tanece Brooks - Tartufu - Tennessee (TN) - Terrann Connor - Terry Dimmick - Tevin Hill -Theresa Christian - Thomas Ally - Thomas Faßnacht - Thomas Werner - Tiana Scott - Tiffany R Engle - Tiger Crab Studios - Tim Fielder -Timi - T.J. Bowdell - T.J. Pulliam - Tmomas - Tob ted and Chocolate City Comics - Todd Slawsby - Tom Johnson - Torsten Sawalies - Towelman - Th atum & Shanesh Brooks-Tatum - Travis Pulley - Trevor Hofvendahl - Ty Hudson - Tyler Ford - Vasco Brown - Vicki V. Hoffman - Wally Hastings - Walter Ostlie - Warren Lapworth - Wayne Riley - wesofthedead - Will McConnell Simpson - Will Sanborn - William Sims - W.J. Hayes - Yari Wildheart - Ymmy - Yosu Gurung - Yurii "Saodhar" Furtat - Zahir Oluwaseyi - Ziki Nelson